Exploring Stone Walls

Exploring Stone Walls

A FIELD GUIDE TO STONE WALLS

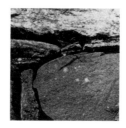

Robert M. Thorson

WALKER & COMPANY

NEW YORK

First published in the United States of America in 2005 by
Walker Publishing Company, Inc.

Published simultaneously in Canada by Fitzhenry and Whiteside,
Markham, Ontario L3R 4T8

For information about permission to reproduce selections from
this book, write to Permissions, Walker & Company,
104 Fifth Avenue, New York, New York 10011.

Library of Congress Cataloging-in-Publication Data

Thorson, Robert M., 1951–
    Exploring stone walls : a field guide to stone walls / Robert M. Thorson.
        p.   cm.
    Includes bibliographical references.
    ISBN 0-8027-7708-2 (pbk. : alk. paper)
    1. Stone walls—New England—History.   2. New England—
Antiquities.   I. Title.
TH2249.T4596   2005
693'.1—dc22

                                                2004053647

Visit Walker & Company's Web site at www.walkerbooks.com

Book design by Mspaceny

Printed in the United States of America

2   4   6   8   10   9   7   5   3   1

To stone-wall enthusiasts everywhere

Some may know what they seek in school and church,
And why they seek it there; for what I search
I must go measuring stone walls, perch on perch.

—Robert Frost, "A Star in a Stoneboat"

CONTENTS

PART III—WALLS IN SPACE AND TIME

ACKNOWLEDGMENTS

The ideas for this book emerged as answers to questions asked of me since publication of my previous book, *Stone by Stone,* in 2002. About half came from those attending public lectures or listening to call-in radio shows. The other half were what I call "Dear Dr. Thorson" letters of inquiry sent to the Stone Wall Initiative, asking for suggestions and advice. People wanted to know what to do to get more information, where to go, and how to name stone walls. After a year or so of this, several booksellers suggested that I write a guide to New England stone walls.

Eventually I dropped what I was doing, began to compile and organize my answers, drove thousands of miles in search of stone, took over a thousand photographs, and gave serious thought to the naming of walls. *Exploring Stone Walls* is the result.

Thanks to everyone, especially the booksellers, who prompted and encouraged me to take the time to write the first "detective" book on stone-wall science. Once I got started, it became lots of fun. Thanks also to the innkeepers and friendly folk who put me up during my two-year odyssey around the back roads of New England. Thanks to my wife, Kristine Thorson, for allowing the family station wagon to be dedicated to the task and for navigating the way. Thanks to Rufus Frost and David Morse for reviewing an early version of the text, and to Kristin Lammi and Nick Bellantoni, for reviewing the stone-wall classification. Thanks to my agent, Lisa Adams, and to the staff at Walker & Company, particularly my editor, Jackie Johnson. Most importantly, thanks to the countless unnamed New Englanders whose collective wisdom about stone walls, freely given, is summarized in these pages.

INTRODUCTION

Old stone walls are keys to the past. Each unlocks a separate door to the American experience. Some walls are tumbled ruins of rounded cobbles. Others are well-maintained historic fences, capped by quarried slabs. Some were built by the first colonial settlers. Others are being built today, in the folk-art traditions of the past.

Beneath such obvious differences are thousands of other clues to the who, what, where, when, and why of New England's stone walls, especially the old, tumble-down walls stranded in its parks, suburbs, and towns as if they were so many ship-wrecks. This guide will show you how to use these clues to observe stone walls more carefully, whether from your kitchen window, your car, or outdoors as you touch, examine, scrutinize, and even smell them. This guide will also show you how to name and classify walls and other stone ruins, then use that knowledge to help understand your own favorite stone wall and how it compares to others in the region.

Anyone can become a stone-wall detective. No tools or special training are needed. Come join me as we follow the trail of clues that weaves back and forth into natural history, American history, geography, and landscape architecture.

If you don't know the age of a stone wall, there are ways to guess. Look at its lichen cover, at the spread of its base, at the graininess of surface stones, and for telltale signs of rebuilding; all are chronological clues. If you want to know a wall's original purpose, you can note how tall or wide it is, search for human tool marks on the stones, then probe for a rubble interior. To name a wall you will look for certain things, then match them to the diagnostic features of the book's classification system. To understand why any stone wall looks the way it does, you need to know three things: the composition of the local bedrock, the behavior of the glacier at that spot, and a simple version of the local cultural history.

As a stone-wall tourist, you may pay new attention to the walls in the backdrop of your vacation scenes. Or you might make a special trip to see the black-and-white zebra walls of Vermont's quartz-rich slate country; the dappled gray granite

Ornate quarrystone wall, West Hartford, Connecticut

walls of southern New Hampshire; the gold-tinted lace walls on Martha's Vineyard; the orderly, straight-edged fieldstone walls within fifty miles of common borders between Connecticut, Rhode Island, and central Massachusetts, the epicenter of traditional New England stone walls. There are maps, lists, classification keys, and other materials to help you explore stone walls anywhere, and at whatever level of expertise you choose. Once you get the hang of it, you begin to see stone walls in many different ways, as scrapbooks of local history, habitants for furtive creatures, art galleries for lichens, ferns, icicles, and fallen leaves, and archives of a deep geological past.

PART I

A CLOSER LOOK AT STONES

Variety in stone size, shape, and composition in a local mix, eastern Connecticut

CHAPTER I

LIFE AND HABITAT

When we encounter a stone wall in the deep woods, we instinctively think of the place as being desolate. This is an illusion. Every stone in every wall is animated with life. On the outside, the stones are painted by microbes, stained by fallen leaves, and crusted by lichens. On the inside, especially near their bases, stone walls are filled with roots and humus, within which live a myriad of creeping creatures. Surrounding walls are the herbaceous vegetation and trees of the forest and human signs of suburban and rural life. Every wall is part of the broader habitat in which we, and other animals, live our lives.

Walls, especially abandoned walls, are an integral part of a woodland ecosystem, often teeming with life. Winter and summer come to walls as well. During winter, the life they contain appears dormant at first glance. But a closer inspection reveals countless tiny tracks in the snow that document the comings and goings of small mammals through the miniature caves between the stones. In summer, walls are brimming with plant and animal life, the lichens and moss flashing different shades of green, based on the moisture they absorb from the air and rain.

One of my small daily

Woody debris on granite fieldstone blocks, inland Maine

Velvet moss limited to one stone, eastern Connecticut

pleasures is watching the colors change on a single roadside boulder protruding from a wall in my neighborhood. During the winter, the stone is a constant brownish gray. From March to December each year, however, its exterior surface swells and shrinks with the changing temperature and humidity, and its color goes from pale greenish gray to the verdant green of fresh grass, then back to the dark green of hemlock before winter comes anew. All of this takes place on the surface of the stone, signs that the wall is alive with bacteria, algae, and lichen throughout the changing seasons.

Many forms of plant and animal life inhabit even the most remote stone walls. A specked crusted coat of lichens is virtually ubiquitous on historic walls. Green stones, when their color is not due to mineral composition, indicate the presence of algae. Black-varnished stones—like their counterparts from desert pavements, or those within volcanic vents—contain a universe of unknown bacteria. Rough and porous stones provide footholds for clinging plants; fractured stones allow roots to grow inward. Voids between the stones provide homes; smaller cracks and crevices, a three-dimensional maze for a myriad of creatures to scurry about. Below the base are the dens of larger burrowing animals—woodchucks being the most familiar.

Above the stone is a canopy of plants impacting on stone walls. Although limbs and entire trees occasionally fall on and damage walls, more commonly walls are benevolently decorated by the gentle falling of autumn leaves. The remains of squirrel lunches and the droppings of birds also add transient color.

Old walls in the deep woods, slowly disintegrating with age, enhance the biodiversity of our woodlands. They are as wild as the life they contain.

MICROBES, FUNGI, AND LICHENS

Stone walls are dusted daily with pollen, which can come from far away. Though visible only at certain times, pollen arrives all year, bringing with it a rain of organic matter that gets caught in the rough world of the rock surfaces. There it becomes food for microbes, and these microbes change the color of the stone—visible manifestations of an otherwise invisible process. In sandy pine forests, during early summer, the walls are painted a light yellow with pine pollen.

Microbes include those forms of life too small to see except beneath a microscope. Though normally restricted to bacteria, mildew, and algae, they also include single-celled animals and plants, the best known of which are the amoebae, which glide unseen over many a wet stone.

The colorful crusts on stones are the byproduct of life on their surfaces. Algae are most conspicuous because they flash green when wet— the color of a nutrient-laden farm pond—then die back to dull brown. The stones most susceptible to an algal coat are those that are porous, meaning that they can hold moisture to wick it out later, or deeply shaded, as beneath hemlock branches in moist

Smooth quartzite boulders, which are usually bare of life

Marble accidentally dissolved into a human face, southern Vermont

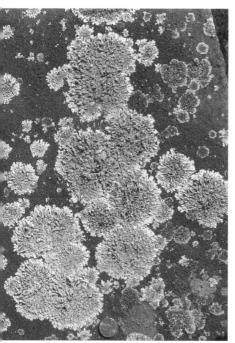

Lichen on quarrystone, Rhode Island

Fungus at the base of a wall, eastern Connecticut

streamside groves. Bacteria help produce the black to purple-black varnish on stones.

Fungi—mushrooms and their kin—often inhabit stone walls. Technically, these are not plants; they don't photosynthesize but obtain their nutrients from the organic material on walls, such as dead leaves. When mushrooms pop up, what we see is only a small portion of what is taking place underground. Mushrooms are principally reproductive devices, curious bits of color in the form of toadstools, puffballs, bracket fungi, and odd coatings of colorful slime. Unable to photosynthesize, they are free to develop any color they like, providing the most vivid tints in stone walls, from bright oranges to iridescent purples.

Lichens are the most conspicuous life form on walls. Most lichens are symbiotic colonies of green algae with fungi. (Technically, they are lichenized fungi.) The fungi provide the structural support and the moist environment required for the algae to photosynthesize. In return, the algae provide the energy for fungal growth and metabolism. In some rare lichens the fungi have a relationship with cyanobacteria, a form of life dating back billions of years, and which was responsible for oxygenating Earth's atmosphere.

There are three basic kinds of lichens on stone walls, based on external appearance.

The hardiest are the *crustose* lichens, which are little more than dots of color on rock surfaces. These closely resemble patches of gum pressed onto sidewalks, adhering so tightly to the stone that they cannot be scraped off. In the arctic, and above the tree line, crustose lichens grow very slowly; the oldest, in the barren lands of north Sweden, are about ten thousand years old. In forested lands, however, their rates of growth are much faster and much more complex, rendering the dating of surfaces by algae growth very difficult. Nevertheless, a conspicuous colony of crustose lichens indicates that the stone in a wall is no longer fresh from the quarry or muddy field.

Foliose lichens are the most familiar. Though attached firmly to the stone at their bases, they grow outward from the stone to form what look like odd, crinkled leaves, usually grayish green in color with variations to milky, pastel, and olive. There are, however, many other colors, principally browns and dark purples, with a few oranges and reds thrown in for fun. Usually the vivid colors associated with foliose lichens are the fruiting bodies, which produce spores that drift in the wind until they catch hold and grow into lichens. When foliose lichens are dry, they crunch beneath your boots, as if you were walking on corn flakes. When wet, they expand and become squishy, like patches of waterlogged velvet.

A third type of lichen is the stalked (or branching) variety, which includes reindeer moss (not a moss) and pixie cups. So closely do some resemble miniature trees that they are still used as scale models for train sets and architectural models. This group of lichens "roots" in low wet places on a base of organic matter, often along with moss. Typically they adorn the low spots lining the center of rubble-topped double walls, growing as if they were a miniature forest in a valley between mountain-sized stones.

The chief significance of lichens with respect to stone walls is the beauty they add, principally of color and texture. Lichens also make the wall a combination of life and rock rather than simply rock. Their beauty is rhythmic, pulsating day and night, sunlight and storm, wet and dry spells, year after year. Many lichens are bleached ashen gray in the winter, then switch to green in summer. Sometimes a wall that is inconspicuous when dry will bloom with vibrant color after a shower.

Certain species of lichen will grow only on certain rock types. As such, an odd-looking lichen often announces an oddly composed stone. It is a clue to investigate the stone more carefully. A less aesthetic but more important function of lichens is to decompose the stone. However pretty they might appear, every lichen produces acids and other complex chemicals (chelating agents) that dissolve stone over time. For all but the most smooth and sterile stones, the layer of lichens and microbes is as complete as a coat of paint. Very few remain uncolonized.

PLANTS

More primitive than the so-called higher (or vascular) plants, moss has been growing on stones since the Paleozoic. Lacking the cells required to pump water very far, mosses require a moist, usually shaded environment, most often on the boundary between the basal stones of a wall and the debris and fallen stones to the side, its flanking apron. When present on a wall, however, they are unusually beautiful, appearing on some stones as if they were green shag carpets or patches of fuzz. More often than not, the stones moss live on are those that can absorb moisture in their pores. Moss changes color as well, from dark drab green to the brightest greens on walls, depending on the availability and timing of moisture.

Ferns are a link between mosses and the higher plants. Though once more abundant in most habitats, today ferns have been outsmarted and outpaced by flowering

Shaggy moss resembling a hairpiece, coastal Maine

plants. The significance of ferns to stone walls is that they are often the most common plants at the boundary between wall and forest floor, taking advantage of the coolness and dampness often present, at least at one side of the wall. In the spring, fronds rise through the soil and shoot upward like asparagus before unrolling, then spreading and obscuring nearby stone walls for most of the summer before dying back in the fall.

The presence of ferns is the most obvious indicator for microclimatic differences in the vicinity of stone walls. Even in more arid areas of New England, the soil near walls is often wetter and cooler, and more likely to support ferns. If one side of the wall has more ferns, you can surmise that that side stays more moist.

Many odd, primitive plants are associated

with stone walls: lycopods (commonly known as princess pine), liverworts, and sphenopsids (horsetails). These holdovers from the Paleozoic remind us that life has been around nearly as long as the stone has.

Most of the other plants in the vicinity of stone walls are flowering plants. Most flowering plants have existed only a few tens of millions of years. Nonwoody flowering plants are often referred to as herbaceous vegetation, which includes grasses as well as what most people consider true flowers. Most of these are annuals, which complete their life cycle within one growing season, reseeding themselves each year. Perennials, which live more than one year but die back to the ground in the fall, are also common.

The flowers associated with stone walls are often more interesting and varied than those elsewhere on the woodland floor or in the yard, for three important reasons. First, the wall creates dramatic differences in microclimates, and therefore microhabitats, depending on landscape position and season. Dry-adapted flowers such as daisies have a better chance on one side (generally the south or west), and shade-tolerant flowers such as impatiens on the other. A second reason is that walls are homes to plant-eating animals that may eat one species but not another, or cache the seeds of one particular plant, thus acting as a force of natural selection that does not operate away from walls.

A third reason that walls and flowers have complex relationships is the historic legacy of human plantings. Many stone walls once formed the edges of gardens and building foundations, against which bulbs and other perennials were planted. After abandonment, even long after wood-frame houses and barns have decomposed, some of these decorative plants remain, reproducing year after year. This

Flowers growing between quartz boulders, Hudson Valley, New York

is well illustrated by clumps of lilac still sprouting from an old cellar hole, or perhaps by patches of daffodils growing along the base of a wall in the woods. Such plants are living fossils of a time when the wall was part of an active farm.

Trees have an enigmatic relationship to stone walls. On the one hand, their weedy growth on abandoned farmsteads has often converted useful architecture to evocative ruins. On the other hand, trees falling during windstorms are the number-one killer of walls, smashing into them when they fall nearby or brushing their stones away with branches when they fall from a distance. Fallen trees often continue to grow, their trunks merging with the stones as if swallowing them.

Trees also shower walls with deadfall debris. Twigs, branches, cones, and bark fall erratically. Needles and leaves provide a seasonal veneer, especially during autumn, when many walls are buried (or nearly so) in fallen foliage. Each autumn crop of leaves and needles is later blown or washed off the wall, enriching both sides with organic matter, which then decomposes. Over time, the extra dose of organic material on both flanks produces a rich mulch that encourages the growth of tree seedlings, which then spread at the base as they mature, their roots eventually pushing or tipping sideways even the most massive stone walls. Another enemy nourished by this mulch are the vines that pull walls apart like so many fingers. Sometimes one side of the wall is enriched more than the other; leaves blown by the prevailing wind may pile up on one side, or all manner of woody debris may be caught on the upslope side of walls after torrential rains.

Trees can also transform walls without touching them, principally by the shade and shelter from winds that they offer, and to a lesser extent by wicking soil moisture into the air, where the humidity helps break down stones. When trees are absent, walls are sunnier, windier, and drier, and thus more variable in temperature than those protected by forest groves. Under the summer canopy of trees, the moister forested wall encourages denser undergrowth plants, which increase stone decomposition, whether by direct dissolution of the minerals, or by encouraging the growth of lichens and moss, both of which enjoy a dietary supplement of dissolved stone. The humidifying effect of the forest also contributes to the destruction of walls by frost. Drawn to the base of the wall during winter freezes, frost swells the soil unevenly, tipping the wall this way or that until it collapses.

The pattern of growth of some trees is even influenced by the presence of stone walls. Three specific cases are especially interesting. The first type is called a line tree; years ago a row of trees, usually maples, would be planted along property lines. Throughout the northeastern woodland there are dozens of enormous, dead line trees with widespread, branching limbs, and whose bark has long since rotted away. They died of old age, surrounded by the vigorous growth of the subsequent species—ash and beech and pine—that took root when the pastures and fields were abandoned. Some line trees were deliberately planted along the edges of cleared fields to provide shade for cattle, as well as to produce sap for maple sugar. Others were planted as part of the architecture of the boundary. The presence of a wall, especially along the boundary between cleared and un-

Nut husks left by squirrels, eastern Connecticut

cleared woods, helped to nurture these trees as they grew; the extra moisture, wind protection, or shelter allowed the seedling to mature beyond the stage where it would have been food for deer, cattle, rabbits, or other herbivores.

Nut trees also have a special association with stone walls. Unlike line trees, however, these actually sprout within the wall and its rubble, where small mammals, notably chipmunks and squirrels, cache nuts. There, the nuts sprout, become trees, which eventually destroy the wall.

Hemlocks thrive in moist, shady ravines and narrow valleys, the same places where thousands of small water-powered mills—sawmills, gristmills, seed mills, and grinding mills—were "seated," and where mill ponds were constructed by early settlers. After such waterworks were abandoned, the same trees returned. You still may find stone walls amid hemlock groves near old mills.

ANIMALS

Each wall is a local habitat, with a flora and fauna distinct from that of the adjacent field. Some of the difference is due to the fact that stones create opportunities lacking on the otherwise fibrous and moist forest floor, being hard, impervious surfaces. But most of the differences are due to the fact that walls change the microclimate of the ground, to which animals respond.

The signature animals for stone walls are chipmunks. Walls make such good habitats for them that they number in the thousands where unmolested by predators, in such off-limits places as Quabbin Reservoir, in the center of mainland Massachusetts. From my kitchen window, which overlooks a stone wall, I have seen not only chipmunks but also mice, rats, gray squirrels, red squirrels, groundhogs, cats, puppies, ferrets, possums, skunks, and raccoons. They use this tumbledown wall as a raised road for traversing the forest floor. Clearly, small mammals love stone walls, as did their burrowing ancestors during the age of the dinosaurs. Field ecologists have discovered that small animal traffic, principally of reptiles and field mice, is much higher on a wall than in its adjacent field, and much higher still on wall intersections. Much the same is true with human traffic on roads and road intersections.

Human traces, especially the rusted tool fragments and old bottles left behind by those who built the walls, may be found in the crevices of many stone walls. When such walls are rebuilt, this residue is often extracted and placed on top of the wall, as if to advertise its treasury of antiques. Children, who find stone walls irresistible to touch, climb, and jostle, use the spaces between stones as vaults for safekeeping toy trucks, small action figures, and dolls. All of my children loved them, especially a wall's crevices and cracks.

Amphibians are surprisingly common around walls. Salamanders appreciate fallen stones, beneath which are moist dark voids in which to rest, each a critter-sized cave. On cool days, they creep around inside the mazework of voids, snatching insects and worms. Toads are more prominent because they often sit directly on the stones, warming in the sun, camouflaged by their color, a perfect match for lichen-mottled granite.

A Civil-war era statue shows a mix of culture and stone, Hudson Valley, New York

Reptiles are furtive dwellers in stone walls. Only once have I seen a rattlesnake in a wall, though they used to be much more common in the colonial era, before bounties were placed on them. In modern times, brown snakes are the most common reptiles I have seen on walls, except where they cross small wetlands, where turtles often sun themselves on the stone. Birds, which share a common ancestry with reptiles, enjoy walls as well, especially those on the edges of clearings, where they provide a place to perch and watch. Perching birds often fly down from the canopy to pick up a seed or an insect, which are more visible on the stone than on the ground.

Spiders, centipedes, pill bugs, ground beetles, and ants live on or near stone. Their abundance can be confirmed simply by turning over any stone in the flanking apron; these little creatures will scurry away, back to the nearest stone.

A freshwater snail in a crevice, Holyoke, Massachusetts

Gastropods—snails and slugs—occupy walls as well. I often see glistening slug trails on the stone, and occasionally an abandoned snail shell. Slugs and snails are often attracted to the algae that grows on smooth stones; scraping up this green film with rasping "teeth" in their tongues, as their counterparts, the periwinkles, do in tidal pools, they lick rocks clean.

We must not forget that many walls are built at the edge of the sea. Crabs and many other tidal creatures inhabit such walls, most of which were installed to prevent erosion.

SEASONS

New Englanders appreciate four distinctive seasons. Stone walls have seasons as well, though they are slightly out of phase with our normal experience. Like the

A shoreline seawall in summer, Isleboro, Maine

negative to a photograph, walls are most visible when life is most invisible. Typically this occurs in January, when snow frames the wall from bottom to top, and when the strengthening, crystal-clear sun casts strong shadows. At this time of year, the upright face of the wall catches more sun and wind than the ground, clearing it of snow. Simultaneously, the drying winter wind and the cold temperature forces life on the stones into remission, rendering them darker. From a distance, stone walls resemble fallen, lifeless gray tree trunks. Winter walls remain well exposed in February and early March, though we notice them less because we've gotten used to them, and because the skies are more often gray.

Our awareness of winter walls diminishes steadily until early spring, then drops dramatically as our attention shifts toward living things, to crocuses and daffodils rather than mud. Next, the greening up of the grass starts with a hint, then a lush low sward rapidly highlights the edge of the wall. As the sward grows higher, it eclipses the walls from below. The leaves of the trees emerge in April and

A fieldstone wall in winter, eastern Connecticut

May, obscuring the walls by dappling them in shade, making the stones harder to see.

In early summer, we can see stone walls well again, not because the understory has died back, but because the gray walls give us visual relief from the ubiquitous greenery. Again, our attention is drawn to stone. Then in late summer the walls, especially where the sunlight strikes, seem alive. Each rainstorm intensifies the growth plastered on walls; algae, lichens, and moss absorb moisture, puff up, and become almost iridescent green.

It is only when the leaves begin to fall that we lose track of the walls again. Lichens are less active, owing to diminished light and to cooler temperatures. The forest canopy pulls our attention upward, where the leaves of deciduous trees blaze with orange and red as their leaf sugars disappear before they drop. Then, to add insult to injury, when the leaves fall, they physically bury the walls along their bases in a giant fluff.

Leafless vines in fall, western Connecticut

Only after the leaves have been dulled to brown, soaked by dreary rains, and pressed to the ground (a thick snowfall that subsequently melts really helps) do we see walls well again. The walls of November are striking, until their novelty fades. They remain this way until they become framed in snow once more, thus beginning another cycle.

January, August, and November are the best wall-watching months in southern New England. For the north woods, it would be December, July, and October. The presence or absence of life drives the annual show of stones.

CHAPTER 2

STONE SIZE AND SHAPE

Every stone is a chip off the old block, a fragment born from the parent crust of the Earth, then subjected to its own personal history. As with children—even identical twins—no two stones are exactly alike. Each has its own size, shape, composition, birthplace, and birth order. In this chapter, we explore the relationship between rock and stone: how to describe them, how to recognize the clues they contain, and how to call each stone by its proper name.

Rock, derived from the Latin *rocca*, refers to the bedrock crust of the Earth. Stone, derived from the Latin *stilla*, "drop," refers to a small piece of the Earth's crust, one of many "drops" from its bedrock "bucket." Rock is a material—stone is an object. To avoid confusing the terms *rock* and *stone*, I offer this simple rule of thumb: The smaller it is, the more changed it is from the original condition, and the more useful it is (or could be), the more it deserves to be called a stone, rather than rock.

For this reason we use the word *cobblestone* rather than *cobblerock;* small rounded pieces of the Earth's crust represent significant departures from the primitive state. Conversely, we wouldn't use the term *gem rock* to describe the diamond set in a ring, or *grave rock* to describe

Naturally formed stone tablets up to twenty feet long, coastal Maine

an engraved marble headstone, because they are both useful and regular in shaped, significant departures from their primitive state. The material taken from a quarry is called stone, though the quarry itself is composed of rock.

The jutting, wave-beaten headlands of Rockport, Massachusetts, and Rockland, Maine, are correctly named because they both expose the rock-hard viscera of the Earth. Equally well named is Stony Brook, Long Island; it doesn't have exposed bedrock, but it does have a concentration of large stones created when the brook cut down through the sandy, boulder-studded glacial ridge. Also well named is Stonington, Connecticut, whose coastal headlands are not very prominent, yet whose soils are ubiquitously littered with glacially transported stones.

The tension between the words *rock* and *stone* explains why the term *rock wall* is used in some places (for example, southwestern Maine), and *stone wall* in another (as in Westchester County, New York). The latter is the clear favorite because stone walls are, by definition, made of fragments of the Earth's crust, rather than of outcrops, and because they are often small and well shaped for human use. The term *rock wall*, however, is fairly common, because there are many areas where the "stones" are large, blocky, and irregular. Hence, the term *rock wall* connotes material chaos just barely constrained by the order imposed by a line of stone. The term *stone wall* connotes more order, principally in the shape and size of the stone.

The word *boulder* derives from the Old Norse *bullersten*, literally "noise stone." These are large rocks that are worn and rounded by wear and weathering. A slab of rock, regardless of size, is not a boulder unless its corners have been rounded by time. Rounded stones on bedrock ledges can often be

A glacial erratic on an ice-scoured ledge, eastern Connecticut

tipped back and forth, resulting in a low, rumbling noise. These are called "thunderstones" in New England, and are alleged to have been used as communication devices by the Indians, not unlike the use of drums and smoke signals farther west.

BIRTH OF STONES

The means by which stones are born can be seen by picking up any stone, unless it is perfectly rounded. Its most prominent feature will probably be the planar fractures outlining two or more of its sides. These fractures or joints cut right through the rocky mass itself, through the beds, folds, and veins that might be present, sometimes even through large mineral crystals. These joints are mechanical fractures, which formed as the rock cracked apart after it cooled. Without them the Earth's surface would be as seamless and rigid as a billiard ball, merely corroded by the chemical processes associated with soils.

Small fractures in slate leading to small fragments, Rhode Island

Joints are the birthmarks of stones. Nearly all of New England's rock was created miles below the surface, where the raw materials baked under enormous pressures for millions of years, eventually forming a solid, continuous mass. At such depths solid rock is so hot and confined that it behaves somewhat like bread dough being kneaded by colossal forces; it can be stretched and folded and squished without breaking. Near the surface, however, the same material is cooler and less confined. Under these conditions, rock behaves as a familiar brittle solid. Though still strong, it will crack apart and break cleanly when the stress becomes too great.

Enormous stress is easy to find inside the Earth, and can have several causes. The simplest is shrinkage, as when hardened lava contracts as it cools. Normally the expansion and contraction of rock occurs at a depth of a mile or so in the Earth's crust, usually in the presence of additional horizontal stresses applied by tectonic motions. Caught up in this giant squeeze machine, blocks of rock the size of counties and towns are splintered sideways even as they expand upward. No large mass of rock can survive intact the stresses coming at it from all directions. As a result, the whole mass breaks up along lines of force, producing—snap, crackle, and pop—millions of joints, which often intersect at acute and obtuse angles.

The blocks between the joints, which are often geometrically regular, are destined to become stones, but they must first be liberated from their places of origin. In New England, the greatest liberator of all was glacial action, which plucked them up from the faces of countless ledges and scattered them about. But the breakup along joints didn't end there. Long after the ice receded, the blocks continued being broken up along the joints by more superficial agencies: frost, gravity, and human ingenuity.

Bedrock: jointing in hard quartzite, Hudson Valley, New York

Joints dictate the shape of every stone. Typically, there are three sets of joints. Joints that are perpendicular to each other produce stones that have right-angle corners and look like cardboard boxes of various shapes. When the joints intersect at angles, the stones form three-dimensional parallelograms. Widely spaced joints yield large stones, and vice versa.

When the glacier came down from the north, it plucked up the previously broken fragments and scattered them about. The best way to imagine how New England's stones came to be distributed in the fields of nearly every farmer is to imagine that each outcropping of bedrock was like a box of sugar cubes with the cardboard sides removed. The hand of the glacier was first pressed firmly down on the top of the pile, but then it began to move slowly forward, pushing the cubes forward, scattering and crushing them in the process, leaving behind a

Large fractures in granite leading to large blocks, Rhode Island

granular residue. Twenty thousand years ago, the weight of the glacier pressed down on broken-up ledges, dragging forward blocks of jointed rock, many of them being crushed into sand. The size, shape, and angularity of practically every stone in every wall is the result of the interaction between broken ledge and ice.

SIZE OF STONES

Some stones are the size of an automobile; others are no larger than a matchbox. The size of the largest stone in a wall is an important clue to local history. If stones are no larger than a man can carry, they signify no more than the lifting and tossing of debris from a pasture. If they are enormous, however, they were moved and assembled into the wall as a construction project, built with teamwork, engineering, and ingenuity.

To geologists and engineers, the terms *boulder, cobble,* and *pebble* have very specific meanings. A boulder is any stone larger than 256 millimeters (mm)—about ten inches—measured across the intermediate diameter. A cobble is anything smaller than 256 mm but larger than 125 mm, about five inches. Everything smaller than that, but larger than 2 mm, is considered a pebble. Unfortunately, there are no standard terms for stone sizes larger than ten inches. All are boulders if somewhat rounded, or something else if not.

With respect to interpreting stone walls, the weight of the stones—relative to the strength it would take a person to lift them—is the way I prefer to describe the size of stones used in walls. The more rounded and smooth a stone of any size is, the easier it is to roll, but the harder it is to lift and transport. Some stones, especially those of volcanic origin, are notably heavier than others of the same size. Keeping these distinctions in mind, I recommend five size categories based on ease of movement: residual stones, assisted stones, two-handers, one-handers, and pebbles.

A residual stone is one that wasn't moved at all, presumably because it was too large. Normally, stones larger than a couch or a small car were left in the field or pasture. (This, of course, depended on the determination of the landowner to get rid of the stone, and to the stone-removing technology available.) Many were later blasted with dynamite, or split in the field by drilling, then moved to the edge of the field on rollers, pulled by oxen, horses, or powerful tractors.

Quarried slabs of granite in an old staircase, northern New Hampshire

An assisted stone is too large to be lifted and carried by one or two people, but small enough to be moved with some contrivance of engineering and/or livestock power. These are the large boulders present at the base of many walls, most of which were skidded or tipped end over end to the edges of fields on stone boats, then rolled and levered into place. Sometimes the marks of the tools used to move stone—jacks, hooks, chains, pry bars—can be seen, providing clues to how the farmer did his work. The presence of assisted stones in a wall demonstrates the determination of a landowner to clear the fields, beyond what was necessary for pasturing.

Smaller than these are stones that could be moved by a single person unassisted. A two-hander is watermelon sized and would require the use of both hands to lift and move it; two-handers are generally synonymous with boulders. One-handers, especially when rounded, are technically cobbles or very small boulders,

Large round boulders forming a single-stone wall, Acadia, Maine

Small flat stones made into a mailbox, Jamestown, Rhode Island

small enough to be lifted and chucked with one hand—no larger than a cantaloupe or acorn squash. One-hander slabs are the size of books, whereas those that are rounded are often called stone potatoes, and fit in the palm of your hand. When one-handers are grainy and jagged, especially when considered as a group, they were often dubbed rubble.

The most primitive wall is a stack of two-handers, especially if they are angular or slabby in shape. Such walls require very little in the way of planning or execution, sometimes nothing more than manual transport, either directly from the field, or to and from a vehicle of some sort. The absence of assisted stones in a wall suggests a limited commitment to clearing the land, which in turn suggests that the farm never reached a stage of wealth and leisure sufficient to justify removing the stone. On pioneering farmsteads, farmers often worked around their assisted-size stones with scythes and rakes and hoes. More rarely, the absence of assisted stones in a wall means there was no livestock to help move the stones.

Both larger (assisted) and smaller (one-hander) stones in a wall indicate that more attention was paid to field clearing, usually at the stage when farms were well established. Large collections of one-handers likely exhibit the work of children. Assisted stones along the base of a wall and two-handers on the top suggest the land was used predominantly as pasture. If assisted stones are within a wall and placed above the ground surface, some mechanical device was used: rollers and ramps were most common, though cranes or moveable derricks were used as well.

This suggests a later date for the wall, usually in the nineteenth century. The complete absence of residual stones in a field surrounded by large assisted stones suggests a major commitment to clear the land of every blemish, which usually took place during the estate stage.

Stone potatoes and rubble heaped on a wall provide a clue to how the land had been used. These stones were too small to be bothered with on primitive farmsteads because they didn't pose a problem for handheld farm implements such as scythes and rakes. Most of the time they would have been left in the field. If they were tossed on a wall, they probably came from an adjacent cultivated field that had been cleared by horse-drawn or tractor-pulled machinery. A farmer would take the time and effort to move the stones because stone potatoes and rubble would break the teeth on the cutting bar of mechanical reapers. However, rubble inside the wall, and surrounded by more well-shaped stone, indicates that the wall was a carefully executed construction project.

THE SHAPE OF STONES

Blocks of rock that broke off the ice sheet and were transported by the ice sheet were essentially angular to begin with and usually large. While moving in the ice sheet, however, their corners were crushed, many were broken down to a smaller size and snapped, scraped, and flaked. The angularity of a stone is the degree to which the corners and edges are still sharp, rather than rounded. An angular stone has fresh, sharp corners. A rounded stone may have remnants of the originally flat surfaces, but no conspicuous corners. A subangular stone is one where corners are prominent, but smoothed at their tips. Conversely, a subrounded stone is like a box with its corners and edges smoothed away.

Wall above a graveyard crypt, preventing soil erosion, western Massachusetts

*   *   *

With respect to New England geology, several basic processes influence the angularity of a stone. All stones are angular when first removed from the bedrock, because the joint planes must intersect in corners and points, producing sharp edges. A milling agency had to act on stone in order for it to become rounded. The most common milling agency was the shear zone at the bottom of the ice sheet, where the stones collided with each other and the bedrock, their edges and corners becoming progressively pecked and crushed away. Normally, this process—even with a uniformly strong stone like granite—will not produce well-rounded stones because they usually become broken before they attain that condition, leaving them subrounded or half rounded. The well-rounded shape, especially if the surface is smooth, usually indicates that the stone has been worn down by the tumbling of moving water in a meltwater stream and/or to a lesser extent along the shoreline of a glacial lake or marine bay. The final process that rounds stones is postglacial weathering. Normally this doesn't work with layered rocks like slate, which can only split into slabs. But on more massive rocks, either within the soil or perched in a stone wall, sharp corners and edges tend to slowly dissolve and disintegrate.

If most of the stones in a stone wall are smooth and well rounded, especially if they are one-handers, they must have washed through a glacial river or along a shoreline. In contrast, if the stones in a wall consist mostly of large angular slabs, they were likely torn loose from a ledge and later released from stagnant ice, never having encountered either a meltwater stream or the shear zone at the base of the ice. A collection of subangular to subrounded stones suggests they were transported in the glacial shear zone, especially if some corners are somewhat rounded and others freshly

Flagstones shaped like books, Berkshires (Lennox), Massachusetts

broken. A collection of subrounded stones is usually the result of short-distance meltwater transport, or particularly effective milling in the shear zone.

For New England farmers, the sphere is the worst possible shape for a stone; it is easy to overlook in the subsoil (waiting to break a plow tip), hard to grub out (its center of mass is deep), difficult to transport on a vehicle (it is likely to roll off), and hard to carry (its center of mass must be held far away from the center of the body). It is also the worst shape from the point of view of wall construction because spheres don't stack well. If spherical stones are present in a wall consisting largely of slabby ones, it usually signifies either holes being plugged or some element of artistic expression. The only advantage of spheres is that big ones can be more easily rolled to the edge of a field with a jack or pry bar.

The geometric proportions of a stone also influence the shape. A stone with equant proportions is one where length, width, and thickness are approximately the same. A column's length far exceeds the other two dimensions, which are roughly equal. In contrast, a tablet has a length and width that are roughly equal, but is very thin. A slab is one where length, width, and thickness are notably different, but not dramatically so. A blade is the rarest; its length is much greater than its width, and its width is much greater than its thickness. They are the antithesis of equant stones.

The combination of a stone's angularity and its geometric proportions gives rise to eight categories of basic shapes common to stones found in New England walls:

- *Blocks* are equant and angular.

- *Balls* are equant and rounded.

- *Prisms* are columns that are angular.

- *Rollers* are columns that are rounded.

Stones in a cairn taking the shape of balls, blocks, prisms, and slabs, western Connecticut

Slabs shaped by tools, then fallen, at the Nathan Hale Homestead in Connecticut

• *Books* are tablets that are angular.

• *Disks* are tablets that are rounded.

• *Slabs* can be either angular or rounded, but are normally subangular.

• *Blades* are usually angular.

These shape categories are directly related to the bedrock type of the stone and the glacial action upon it. This means that you can guess what the stone is made of and what happened to it, even from a distance, even when covered by lichens. Blocks and balls are produced by massive, un-layered rocks, often granite in New England. Balls were usually bounced along in glacial meltwater streams; if they are large erratics, they were rolled great distances at the base of the ice. Blocks occur where massive rocks were crushed, but not milled. Prisms and rollers most often come from chilled lava and, to a lesser extent, from the crests of tight folds in otherwise soft rocks. Books, disks, and thin slabs come from well-layered but fairly strong metamorphic rocks called schist, and from quartz veins in all types of rocks. Thicker slabs come from a variety of rock types, though the majority are thickly banded metamorphic rocks called gneiss. Blades come almost exclusively from strong rocks related to slate that were ripped up but not milled.

The important point is that the shape and angularity of the stone dictates the structural ability of the wall made from it. Balls make the worst walls. Slabs make the best. Books give walls the tightest weave and the straightest fronts. Large blades make the best thrufters, elongated stones placed inside a wall to bind its two sides together.

CHAPTER 3

MINERALS AND ROCK TYPE

Every wall is a collection of rocks. No two are exactly alike. Every rock in every wall is also a collection of minerals, crystals that formed automatically as atoms came together in a certain way, and only that way. Most of the minerals common to rocks in walls—quartz, feldspar, mica, and garnet—are fairly unspectacular, the result of being cooked deep underground during the continental collisions that created New England's rocks. But some minerals are quite unusual, owing to the quirkiness of New England's geological history, which involved more unusual processes such as steaming fissures, lava lakes, sudden earthquake motions, and dinosaur footprints along tropical lake shorelines. A few minerals even form as a result of weathering: common rust, the reddish yellow stain on many rocks, is called limonite, which is made up chiefly of the mineral goethite. Some of the dust that forms on stones during weathering is composed of clay minerals.

Besides having certain minerals, stones also have chemistry, bulk texture, physical properties, structural grain, and weathering features. Geologists use the general term *lithology* to describe the overall composition of rocks and stones, a word deriving from the Greek *logos,* "knowledge," and *lith,* "stone." The term

Geodes, agates, and crystals in a mortared wall, inland Maine

geology derives from the same root for knowledge, but emphasizes the whole Earth rather than only its rocks.

MINERALS

A naturally occurring, inorganic solid with a specific crystalline structure, a mineral's chemical composition is either fixed or varies within well-defined limits. Diamond is one of the simplest minerals, consisting of carbon atoms bound together in a densely packed arrangement; graphite, once used to make pencil leads and now used primarily for machine lubrication, has the same chemical composition as diamond, but its carbon atoms are organized into small sheets that easily slide past one another.

New England has many more minerals than those described here. The region's rocks are overwhelmingly dominated by minerals of the silicate group, in which silicon and oxygen combine with other elements, notably aluminum, iron, magnesium, potassium sodium, and calcium. Next in abundance is the group responsible for limestone and marble, composed chiefly of the mineral calcite, which takes its name from the important element calcium.

The remaining minerals belong to groups dominated by metals. These include the iron oxides, which were the ores for the colonial iron industry; the sulfides, which give rise to crumbly rusty walls; and rarest of all, the native metals—gold, silver, and copper.

The bulk of most rocks within walls is composed of only five mineral groups—micas, garnets, quartz, feldspars, and mafics (described later). All of these can be identified at a glance when the crystals are large, though in most cases the minerals are no larger than a sand grain and are best seen with a small magnifying glass.

Mica occurs in sheets and books, often ranging from the size of a pea to the size of a silver dollar. The most common mica—muscovite—is the bronze-colored, flexible mineral that gleams like gold on freshly broken rocks and puts the sparkle into what might otherwise be drab sand. Most New England mica was created by the slow pressure-cooking of clay and mud that had covered the bottom of the ocean before the land was born.

Garnet usually is present in rocks rich in mica. Fresh garnet crystals may be of gem quality and look like miniature, ruby-colored soccer balls the size of a sand grain or a pea. The reddish purple layers of sand near the high-tide line on beaches are made of garnet as well, though these were crushed into sand by the glacier before being concentrated by waves. Weathered garnets tend to be little more than rusty blotches on otherwise shiny rocks. Garnet is a signature mineral for rocks that were formed in the roots of ancient mountains.

Quartz occurs nearly everywhere in New England. The most beautiful specimens are the transparent, prismatic, six-sided crystals with pointed tips; they can be clear, lavender-colored (amethyst), or smoky in hue. Normally, however, quartz is the grayish, often greasy-looking mineral filling the spaces between other minerals in granite, or the light-colored bands in layered rock. Quartz occurs most dramatically as the hard, milky white veins, layers, and blobs often seen in road cuts, headlands, and ledges, and in most field-stones. Quartz veins are particularly striking in western New England (Taconics, Berkshires, and Vermont), where they are common and contrast strongly with the drabness of the local gray rock.

A quartz vein with visible crystals, coastal Maine

Chemically, quartz consists of silicon and oxygen, bound together in pyramid-shaped units. This makes it especially resistant both to weathering in the soil and to mechanical wear and tear. Hence, quartz is the most common ingredient of sand on the beach. When cemented, it becomes sandstone. When pressure-cooked, quartz becomes quartzite, which is often the hardest rock in New England. A collection of cobbles is often lighter colored than the local bedrock because it contains a higher proportion of resistant, quartz-rich stones.

Feldspar is a large group of minerals, making up perhaps as much as half of all rocks in New England. Basically, the feldspars are the opaque white or pastel-colored (pink, brown, gray) grains within granites that are not mica, garnet, quartz, or dark specks (see below). Feldspar is most easily distinguished from quartz (which is also light colored) because it usually has a grain like that of wood, and always breaks (or cleaves) on regular planar surfaces that reflect light almost as well as mica. There are two important groups of feldspars. The most common are the white, pink, and brown ones that make up the bulk of granite and most slabby layered rock (gneiss). The other ones occur in darker more iron-rich rock, best seen as lath-shaped crystals in dark, hardened lava.

A vast, highly variable group of minerals accounts for the billions of black speckles in many New England rocks. These iron- and magnesium-bearing silicate minerals, prevalent in the Earth's interior, are more rare in its outer crust. Though mineralogy texts divide them into dozens of minerals from several important groups, in this book I lump them into a single category, called the mafic minerals ("ma" for magnesium, "f" for iron, and "ic" for "ferric," the state of iron in the absence of oxygen). Mafic minerals account for most of a stone wall's black speckles. They also make light-colored rocks appear gray from a distance, and the speckles easily rust into the familiar yellowish brown and reddish brown soil colors.

A marble tombstone dissolving, southern Vermont

The silicate mineral called olivine, named for its olive color, accounts for green-tinged rocks that are locally common, especially the very dark and heavy ones. In lighter-colored rocks, the green tint is usually contributed by one or more minerals of the so-called greenschist group, which develops when rocks are only slightly metamorphosed. This type of rock is especially prominent in the younger sedimentary basins of Narragansett Bay, Boston, and the lowlands of western and northern New England.

Finally, the mineral calcite constitutes the bulk of marble, an important New England rock that occurs in a single belt extending from Stratford, Connecticut, through the Berkshires, western Vermont, and to Lake Champlain and beyond. Unlike other light-colored minerals—mica, quartz, feldspar—calcite is not a silicate. Calcite is conspicuous and easy to identify in marble because it has a sugary texture usually accompanied by swirls of gray and pastel stain.

It also is soft (it can be easily scratched with a nail) and highly soluble—calcite often is worn away, forming caves, sinkholes, odd-shaped boulders, and weird weathering surfaces. After being quarried for buildings and gravestones, limestone and marble begin to dissolve, a process apparent in the fading of engraving and other ornamentation. In many New England marbles, the mineral calcite is converted to the mineral dolomite when the element calcium is either wholly or partially replaced by the element magnesium. The new rock is grayer and harder, and therefore much more resistant to weathering.

ROCK TEXTURE

Some rocks are dark and massive, their minerals invisible to the naked eye. Others have gem-shaped mineral crystals, floating like plums in a pudding. Some contain pebbles that have been stretched and bent into odd contortions. Others have a grain, like that of wood, but are made of mica-rich layers. Such differences in the size, arrangement, and layering of minerals create what's called the texture of a rock.

The way a rock was made determines its texture. The first method is when magma deep inside the Earth crystallizes, literally freezing when its temperature falls below its freezing point, which is higher than the freezing point for water. The crystals precipitate first as little grains in a silicate slush that gradually get larger until they fuse together, producing igneous rock with an interlocking texture that stays frozen at temperatures typical of the Earth's surface. A coarse-grained granite provides an ideal example of interlocking texture. Most of it is made of pastel grains of feldspar with irregular blotches of quartz filling in the spaces, as if it were water frozen around grains of sand.

The second simple way to make a rock is to

Interlocking (igneous) texture in granite, Acadia, Maine

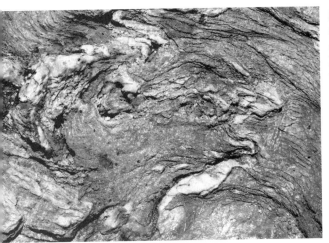

Contorted texture from almost-melted rock (migmatite), central Vermont

glue previously broken pieces of rock together with cement, producing what is called a particle texture. Normally, the cementation takes place deep underground when fluids rich in dissolved minerals migrate between the pores, leaving a glue composed of silica and lime behind. Cemented sand is called sandstone. Cemented gravel is called a conglomerate. Siltstones and shale are examples of particle textures, though the grains are too small to see. A particle texture is only as strong as the bond between its grains; typically these rocks are quite weak because they come apart between the original grains and layers.

The third and most complicated way to make a rock is to change the raw materials in a fundamental way without allowing them to melt. Such rocks are metamorphic rocks, their earlier forms having been "morphed" from their previous condition. The most common way to do this is to pressure-cook the raw material underground; in the process, what might have started as muddy rock can be transformed into a beautifully speckled, often banded rock, full of mica and quartz. This is called a foliated

Particle texture in puddingstone (conglomerate), Rhode Island

texture. Other, less common metamorphic textures are created when rocks are baked as if fired in a kiln, or sheared by earthquake motion.

"Massive texture" is a catch-all category for a rock with no visible texture at all. Such rocks might display one of the previous three textures if viewed microscopically, but if we can't see differences with the naked eye, let's just consider them massive. Lava that cooled too quickly for visible crystals to grow or limestone partially converted to marble are examples of rock with texture too difficult to differentiate in the context of learning about the rocks one finds in stone walls.

ROCK TYPES

Granite froms wherever previous sediments were pushed deep underground, where they completely melted, then were allowed to cool. Normally it has an interlocking texture. Quartz is always present, usually filling the space between pink, yellowish, or gray feldspars. Granite most often has dark mafic specks, and there may be large books of mica. Granite is strong because the crystals fused as they grew together; it is light-colored because its constituent minerals are deficient in iron and magnesium. Because it is massive (rather than foliated), granite lacks a visible grain. It tends to produce blocks rather than slabs. Mechanically strong, granite often creates large fragments; this is why most of the large glacial erratics are granite boulders. When rolled in streams, granite often yields spherical or elliptical shapes.

Basalt—known locally as traprock—is the only other type of igneous rock important to stone walls. Basalt is a nearly black (sometimes dark greenish gray), massive, resistant volcanic rock that weathers to a

Basalt traprock showing ends of prisms, Holyoke, Massachusetts

conspicuous rusty orange color. In most cases, basalt crystallized from lava flows that erupted from fissures during early Jurassic times, when the continent was being rifted apart to create the Atlantic ocean. As the hardened lava cooled and contracted, it became heavily fractured, often in prism shapes up to twenty feet long. Normally, however, the top and bottoms of each flow broke in a much more complicated fashion, producing a jumble of dark, irregular rocks. The frozen lava flows were then tipped eastward, producing elongate ridges as much as four hundred feet above the softer Jurassic sedimentary rocks on either side. Basalt also occurs as vertical ridges that cut through the older metamorphic rock of the eastern and western highlands.

Layered (foliated) metamorphic texture in gneiss, eastern Connecticut

The importance of basalt or traprock to stone walls derives from its unusual weight, mechanical resistance, and chemical behavior. Near the top or bottom of the lava flows, where the pattern of fracture was complex and chaotic, thousands of hard, odd-shaped blocks were produced. In the middle of the lava flows, however, the traprock produced prisms, which rounded off into roller shapes like cordwood logs. Because traprock is strong, these chilled lava blocks tend to survive, even when transported great distances, becoming especially concentrated where other rocks are weak. Since basalt is heavier than other stones of the same size, it is an especially good rock for pressing walls together.

Gneiss is the most common metamorphic rock in New England. Though often similar in mineral composition to granite, gneiss can be recognized as being well layered, with a series of light bands of quartz and feldspar and dark bands of mafic minerals. Hence, whether to classify a particular rock as a granite or a granite gneiss is largely a function of whether the banding is evident. Gneiss forms under prolonged conditions of high pressures and temperatures, often just below the melting point. At such high temperatures, the elements of the original material are free to migrate with the mass, producing all sorts of odd bands and blobs.

The bands in gneiss alternate between resistant (usually granite) and nonresistant (usually richer in mica and mafic minerals) material. This causes the rock to break into slabs often about the size of a briefcase, rather than blocks like most cardboard boxes. When these are moved by the glacier, their edges become rounded into irregular shapes, like foam pillows for a couch. Large boulders are made less often of gneiss than granite, because the layering creates a greater opportunity for the boulder to break during transport. Massive fieldstone walls where the stones appear large and regular in shape are often made of granite gneiss.

Schist is the next down the line of metamorphic conversion. Like gneiss, it is also conspicuously foliated, but schist layers are mica-rich, and display a conspicuous grain like that of wood. Because the layering is so tight, schist usually breaks up into tabular stones similar in size and shape to large books, or laptop computers. During a glacial transport, tablets of schist are usually snapped in half, again and again. When moved by streams, they round into irregular disks.

Associated with ledges of schist are layers that lack any kind of foliation. These are most often quartzite, which formed from more sandy and cleaner sediments than those which made schist. Also present in schist ledges are places where mafic minerals are concentrated. Such ledges produce thin plates and slabs of stone, of variable and often multicolored composition, and their rocks ceate some of the most regular and beautiful stone walls in the region.

Slate is mud that was metamorphosed under temperatures and pressures beyond that needed to make a layered sedimentary rock called shale, but

Layered (foliated) metamorphic texture in slate, Hudson Valley, New York

Mudrock (argillite) below quartz, Hudson Valley, New York

too low to yield schist. Slate is identified by its dark shiny surfaces, which cleave into pieces like chubby placards. The sheen in slate results from microscopic bits of mica, quartz, and clay minerals that are too small to see with the naked eye. In outcrop, slate is usually too soft to produce boulders or even slabs. In places, however, the slate is cemented by dissolved silica, and is therefore both very platy and very resistant to decay.

Mudrock is a catch-all term for black to gray rocks with a massive texture. These are usually called argillite, siltstone, and gritstone when they are derived from volcanic sources, and shale when the dark color is due to organic remains. Weak metamorphism accounts for the greenish tinge found on many of these rocks. Another conspicuous feature is that the original sedimentary layering is often visible, although somewhat deformed. Pebbles, beds of sand, ripple marks, and even bits of petrified wood and coal layers are sometimes present. These dark rocks do not have a characteristic shape. Rather, their shape is governed by almost random fractures caused by whatever tectonic stresses were taking place. What sets them apart are their drab colors and dusky surfaces. Vermont is loaded with such rocks.

Though the term *soft rock* seems counterintuitive, much of far-western New England is underlain by rocks too soft to produce much in the way of boulders. These are sedimentary rocks—thick, monotonous sequences of mudstone, shale, and limestone that have not been significantly metamorphosed. Though not as common, the most conspicuous soft rocks in New England are the Jurassic redbeds (actually brown to maroon) of the Connecticut River Lowland.

Quartzite ranges from gray to clear, and is often slabby. When coarse grained, quartzite has the vitreous sheen of quartz. Essentially, it is a metamorphosed sandstone. The original sand grains were pressed so tightly that the quartz at their tips was transferred to the pores, producing something resembling the interlocking texture of a fine-grained igneous rock. Quartzite is often the strongest rock in a wall because there are no weak minerals or layers.

Conglomerate is essentially cemented gravel, normally gray in color, and resembling concrete made from pebbles, rather than from crushed rock. Called puddingstone by the colonists, this rock type is par-

Soft rock (brown sandstone), central Connecticut

ticularly common on the bedrock headlands in Narragansett Bay, Rhode Island, and in the Boston area. Though conglomerate is typically considered a sedimentary rock, much of it is in New England metamorphosed to the quartzite stage, with the pebbles having become bonded by silica migration and stretched and contorted into usual shapes. Such rocks are more accurately dubbed metaconglomerates.

Marble is a gray to white, unfoliated metamorphic rock composed principally (and originally) of the mineral calcite. Marble is often swirled or streaked with unusual colors caused by chemical impurities. New England marble is generally restricted to a single belt that runs all the way up the Housatonic Valley in western Connecticut, the Berkshires of Massachusetts, and the Valley of Vermont, from Bennington to Lake Champlain. It represents the deep burial and transformation of what were once lime mud and reefs that formed in an environment not that different from the Bahamas today.

Soft enough to be cut with a saw, marble has been widely used for gravestones and monuments. Unfortunately, it weathers to a powdery exterior because it is soluble in rainwater. Since it is also mechanically weak during the crushing process, the marble belt is not rich in stone walls. Where they are present, these walls are usually composed of quarried blocks, or of the residue (tailings) from quarry activity. In many areas marble has been rendered more resistant by "dolomitization," in which the element magnesium has replaced the original calcium in the calcite lattice.

Increasingly common artificial rock, eastern Connecticut

Dolomitic marble is much less soluble and much more resistant, and thus more useful in stone walls.

Artificial stone is widespread in the stone walls of New England. It always amazes me how much broken-up brick, concrete, and remnants of bituminous pavement there is not only on top of roadside and farmstead walls, but within them as well. I suspect the presence of artificial stone is the rule rather than the exception in roadside walls. Synthetic stone, running the gamut from faux granite to faux marble, is also widely used in the building/landscaping industry. The raw material, of course, is usually crushed stone. There is one wall in my town, however, in which the artificial stone is made of moulded plastic. The wall is actually hollow.

THE MIX OF STONES IN A WALL

Far and away the most common source for New England walls historically has been the adjacent fields. The stone was simply plucked from fields and pastures, then skidded, carted, rolled, dragged, or otherwise scuttled aside to the nearest fence line, where later it usually ended up in stone walls. Original fieldstone is stone that has remained on the edge of the field (or the farm) from which it was taken, whereas secondary fieldstone has been moved from its original source to be used elsewhere. Original fieldstone was initially refuse. Secondary fieldstone is, by definition, a resource rather than refuse.

The provenance of fieldstone refers to the place from which it was originally obtained. In the case of fieldstone in glacial country, provenance must be assessed at three separate levels: the bedrock mix, the local mix, and the wall mix.

The bedrock mix describes those stones that could potentially be obtained from nearby outcroppings of bedrock. Typical bedrock mixes are:

- granite and gneiss
- schist and slate
- mudrock and quartzite
- shale and conglomerates

When the collection of stones in a wall accurately reflects the bedrock mix, especially if the stones are angular, we can be fairly sure the rocks were transported by a glacier only a short distance before being released by the melting of stagnant ice.

Layered bedrock yielding a mixture of stone to the wall above it, eastern Connecticut

In contrast, the local mix describes the types of stones found in the glacially transported natural subsoil. The local mix is fairly easy to identify where the fields are littered with excess stone similar to that used in the wall. Sometimes there is little relationship between the local mix and the bedrock mix; for example, a till (or topsoil) rich in slate fragments may lie above a polished granite bedrock. Usually this would indicate either that the local bedrock was too hard to produce many stones, or that a surplus of softer, more erodable rock was dragged in from the north-northwest, the direction from which the glacier arrived. Contrasts between the bedrock mix and the local mix reflect glacial sorting mechanisms. Lodgment till was plastered onto an accreting surface by ice that came from far away; its stones are typically more dispersed and beaten up, having come from a broader, more integrated source area. In meltout till, the stones were let down on the land as the last of the ice melted; its stones are typically more jagged, less scratched, and more concentrated, having come from closer in. Typically, when the local mix resembles the bedrock mix, we are looking at either an abundance of meltout till or lodgment till obtained from weak rocks.

The wall mix is the mixture of stones visible in the wall itself. When it closely resembles the local mix, it indicates that the principal reason for wall construction

Far-traveled stones from Orient Point on Long Island, New York

was stone disposal. When the wall mix differs from the local mix, it suggests some sort of selection process. A common pattern is when the wall mix contains the same composition as the local mix, but a higher proportion of regularly shaped slabs. Such a wall is said to be high-graded. Sometimes the situation is reversed, with the wall mix containing a population of stones that are less suitable for building. Such a wall is said to be low-graded. This usually means that the better stones were pulled for construction projects somewhere else.

As a simple rule of thumb, fieldstone is considered primary when the wall mix resembles the local mix. This, in turn, suggests construction before widespread use of petroleum, when stones were hauled longer distances more readily. When a wall betrays no apparent sorting of stones, especially if the wall is poorly constructed, that suggests it was built long ago by a farmer to dispose of stones. Such walls are most common in New England, and therefore most traditional. Fieldstone is considered secondary when the local mix and the wall mix have different compositions indicating that the stone was moved to the location of the wall chiefly for architectural rather than for agricultural purposes.

Field transport refers to moving stone only as far as the nearest edge of the field, as was done during the pioneering stage of farming. Farm transport refers to movement at the scale of a farm, usually signaled by the culling of fieldstone for well-shaped stones, and their subsequent transport to walls being built nearby. This is a clue that the wall was built after the farm was well established. Export refers to the actual shipment of the stone from one place to another. Export can be deduced when a stone wall lies on soils devoid of stone, or when a stone in a wall can be traced to a source from the south, as glacial transport only occurred north to south. Quarried rock is, by definition, exported stone, as are exotic stones, which are wholly out of place.

For example, a stone wall builder may have picked from the beaches and used ballast stones from all over the globe, offloaded in New England ports before the ships took on heavy material for trade, such as whale oil and timber. Most ballast stones are well rounded. The most easily recognized exotic stones in New England are the waxy gray, often lime-crusted cobbles of flint that litter the shores of the English Channel.

Quarrystone comes from a quarry where it was mined before being hauled to wherever. A surface quarry is a natural concentration of stone, which may or may not occur on a rock outcrop. Stone from a surface quarry can be picked up and hauled away easily, and usually looks weathered. Sometimes a zone of highly concentrated fieldstone, especially in the corner of a livestock pen, has been exploited as a surface quarry.

Quarrystones from bedrock quarries, however, must be dislodged by drilling and/or blasting, activities that leave telltale drill-hole marks on the stone. Walls made of quarrystone often are found near village centers, because village life usually requires more stone, and of a higher quality, than might be available from local excavations and fields. Quarrystone, because of its extra expense, reflects the wealth of the landowner.

Quarried slate, granite, sandstone, and brick, Cape Cod, Massachusetts

Prior to the late-nineteenth century, almost all of the quarried rock in New England came from local quarries. Every village, and many farms, had their own sources of rock, from which were taken the blocks used to build cemetery walls, sea walls, wharfs, and piers. These quarries were typically natural outcrops of granite and gneiss, usually on steep slopes. Stones were harvested using fairly primitive drills, pry bars, and wedges.

Some New England rock was exported much more widely than the nearest village, even before the twentieth century. Vermont marble is probably the most conspicuous quarried rock, occurring as gravestone slabs and the regular-shaped blocks of stone (called dimension stone) used in buildings. The granite quarries of

Uniform quarried slabs,
eastern Connecticut

southern New England, concentrated near Branford, Connecticut, are world-famous. Much of the slate used for early cemetery stones and roof shingles was exported from western New England. Traprock quarries are common now but produce crushed rock for driveways, concrete, and road pavement. The colonists dubbed one type of quarried rock freestone because it could be taken almost without effort from the interbedded sandstone and siltstone strata, and hence lacks the drill holes of other quarried rock. Freestone was present in the Connecticut River Valley (as well as the nearby Newark basin in New Jersey), and to a lesser extent in other sedimentary basins along the Hudson River, in Rhode Island, and near Boston. Brownstone, used to build homes, public buildings, and churches in the Northeast, is composed of freestone, specifically maroon-red slabs of sandstone.

Another type of stone that was free for the taking was rubble leftover from places where rock was blasted, usually for quarries, building foundations, and transportation improvements. Called blast rubble, it is much more irregular in shape than quarried stone, even though it has drill holes and saw marks.

Many walls, especially those around cemeteries and parks, have a hybrid mixture of quarrystone and fieldstone. Usually the proportion of quarrystone corresponds to the proximity of wealth and urban life. The most common hybrid wall is a typical fieldstone wall, with a top course of large quarried slabs as capstones. Another hybrid setting is in fieldstone walls where the ends or terminations are either built of quarried stone or have quarried posts installed vertically for gates or marked entrances.

CHAPTER 4

FEATURES AND MARKS

Many people have brought me odd stones they found in stone walls or in the basements and attics of old properties, wondering whether the stones were rare or valuable. Most people left disappointed. What one person thought was a delicate plant fossil turned out to be an iron and manganese stain from deep brackish groundwater. Someone's hopeful meteorite turned out to be a rounded clump of bog iron. Grooves alleged to have been places where Native Americans straightened the shafts of arrows turned out to be gaps where soluble metals dissolved away from the stone.

Most of the curious features are mechanical marks on stones. The most distinctive are probably the cylindrical, carrot-sized drill holes (actually half holes) left by quarrymen. The most common are glacial marks or striations. But dozens of other unusual marks provide clues to the sequence of bangs, scrapes, scratches, drillings, and poundings that fashioned New England stones from the basic rock, whether by natural or human agency. Usually a single stone has a single mark from a single event. But sometimes multiple marks cut one another. For example, on many stones evidence for polishing

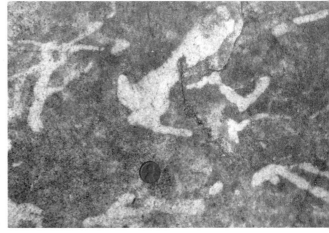

False rock art in granite, Watch Hill, Rhode Island

caused by earthquake activity is followed by nicks from glacial movement, then skid marks made when the stone was hauled to the edge of the field, all cross-cutting each other. A fresh spot on an otherwise weather-beaten surface may show intentional shaping with a hammer or chisel. Such tool marks initiate a new cycle of weathering, as if resetting a clock. In sum, the odd lumps, scrapes, and stains on stones give witness to an intriguing history.

Recognizing and identifying natural curiosities is one of the most enjoyable aspects of exploring stone walls. They help us appreciate that the wall-building process didn't start with human beings, but with the creation of rock in the first place, followed by the making and shaping of the stone by glacial action, human handling, then natural processes once again.

FOSSILS, FOLDS, AND OTHER FEATURES

Remnant of a hole drilled to split granite, western Massachusetts

Fossils are somewhat rare in New England stone, even though most of the material from which the stone was made was originally marine in origin, and often contained oceanic plankton and shells. These fossils were destroyed by the remelting processes deep within the roots of mountains. Fossils remain only in places where the rocks containing them have not been cooked to the extreme. Fossils are present, but rare in the softer, slate-rich and limy rocks of western New England north of Albany and in the Boston and Narragansett Basins. The best fossils, however, come from the reddish brown shale and sandstones of the Connecticut River Valley, and the lowlands of north central New Jersey. They occasionally contain fossil footprints of many kinds of reptiles. One specific footprint, the three-toed, claw-tipped track of the reptile *Eubrontes,* is the Connecticut state fossil. In darker stones, fossil fish, the trunks and branches of primitive trees, and ferns have been found. Glaciation scattered these red sedimentary rocks over much of Massachusetts and Connecticut east of the Connecticut River, giving much broader possibilities for encountering these fossils in stone walls. Every homeowner southeast of Brattleboro, Vermont, may find one in their backyard. Associated with these fossil-bearing red beds are curious marks made by rain, wind, and weather on the sediments as they accumulated: mud cracks, ripple marks, and the impact scars of raindrops.

Accordion-style folds are among the most puzzling finds in wall stone because they raise the question of how solid rock is folded without breaking. When hot and under pressure, rock can be easily folded, distorted, and squished. But once it cools it becomes brittle, and breaks rather than bends. The presence of folds indicates that the rock was subjected to squeezing forces, either compression or sideways shear.

Stones also may have veins, places where material was injected into the host rock. Milky quartz and granite are the most common type of veins in darker rocks and are especially common in the Berkshires and the Green Mountains. Veins of black basalt in light-colored granites are common along the Maine coast. If the vein is straight, the host rock was a brittle solid at the time of rupture and when the vein material squirted into a joint. If the vein is folded, compressed, or otherwise distorted, the host rock was solid but soft when vein material was injected.

A pegmatite is a special type of vein that has unusually large, often gem-quality crystals: quartz hexagons, mica the size of books, tourmaline needles, barite, and lead ores. Rarely, there is a glint of gold and silver. In normal veins, the liquid rock is injected like toothpaste into the host rock.

The folds in gneiss etched out by weathering, eastern Connecticut

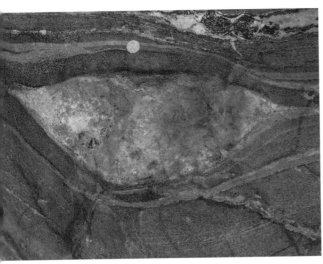

An augen (eye) of quartz in gneiss, eastern Connecticut

In pegmatites, it is the steaming hot vapor and water solutions that move into open fractures, allowing minerals to finish growing with perfect crystal faces intact. Pegmatite quarries in New England have always provided its best gems. Large, pure feldspar crystals have been mined for the ceramic industry.

Augens are special features of gneiss. An augen—from the German word for "eye"—is a clot of light-colored quartz or granite formed usually when a band of soft rock was squeezed sideways into a lump that tapers abruptly on both sides. It can sometimes give the impression that the rock is staring back at you.

Many rocks contain easily seen, well-formed crystals that are larger than those making up the bulk of the rock. These most commonly form when a body of magma has a two-stage cooling history, an interval of slow cooling accompanied by the growth of large crystals, followed by cooling too quick for large crystals to grow. Sometimes the crystals settle to the bottom of the liquid magma, producing layers of large crystals. The most common in New England walls are large, light-colored feldspar crystals suspended either in a mush of granite or in a mass of dark basalt. They also form in mica-rich schists: purple garnets, cubes of pyrite, and crosses of black staurolite are frequently found.

Xenoliths are blocks of the host rock (also called country rock) that melted off the sides of a magma chamber, then fell in. Usually they occur as circular or teardrop-shaped dark spots in granite and display visible rims where the thermal and chemical reactions between the liquid magma and solid fragment took place before final cooling.

Geodes were formed by gas bubbles in volcanic rock that either filled or partially filled with minerals precipitated from groundwater, which was usually hot from the residual heat of the lava. In geodes, the open space preserves the gemlike quality of the crystals and the delicate banding that formed after each blast of hot steam and water. Geodes are like spherical pegmatites.

A geological fault is a jagged tear at the Earth's surface where one piece of land is moving past another. At the scale of a stone, however, faults are flat breaks forced to slide against each other. Usually this can be detected by what looks like a joint surface, but on closer inspection has a curved face and a glistening polished surface with linear streaks called slickensides. When the actual sliding face hasn't been preserved, faults in stones are indicated by distinct layers, veins, or large crystals that were broken along a clean line, then shifted sideways. Each fault is "fossil" evidence of long-quieted earthquakes.

Sometimes the breaks themselves form interesting features. Certainly this is the case with the hexagonal columns that form in the middle of basalt flows as the cooling cracks travel downward. Another type of fracture has the shape of a clamshell. These curved breaks are called conchoidal fractures, from the Greek *konche*, "shell." When small, they indicate the release of concentrated pressure, either from impacts or from glacial pressure. When these fractures are large, they usually indicate the opening of an expansion joint in massive rock from a specific point.

Many other joint surfaces have thick encrustations of purple-black varnish, the precipitation of metals from chemically rich underground water moving through rock fractures. Sometimes the encrustations take the form of branching patterns called dendrites, which look for all practical purposes like fossilized fern leaves. The pattern is the result of the slow opening of the feather edge of a joint, with the mineral crust precipitating as the crack widens.

A curved break from a glacially snapped basalt boulder, eastern Connecticut

GLACIER MARKS

The passage of glaciers over the land produced a variety of marks that are easy and fun to interpret, especially on smooth, dark stones; they are less visible on grainier, rougher rocks that crush more easily. Glacial scratches or striations often form parallel sets of straight lines on the rims and flat surfaces of stones. Some are curved, which means that the stone spun around in the ice as it became caught on the bedrock below. If striations widen as they deepen, the stones were pressed tightly together before becoming stuck. Striations that crosscut each other usually mean that the stone shifted its position between encounters. Striations on only one side of a stone suggest that it was gripped on the other sides—either by the ice or by the silty debris being plastered onto the land below the moving ice. Striations on

only one corner or edge of a boulder indicate that it only briefly touched down on bedrock, before being drawn back up in the glacier.

Bullet stones are a special kind of striated stone. The end that faced upglacier has been ground down to a rounded tip as it was striated away, whereas the downglacier side has remained rough. On bullet stones, the striations parallel the elongate shape of the stone, and resemble the grooves on a bullet caused by rifling of the barrel.

Polished stones can sometimes be found. The polish results from billions of microscopic striations produced by a gritty paste moving over the stone at the interface of ice and bedrock. Sometimes a rock held by the ice plowed into the grit, leaving only its tip polished. More often the grit was smeared over a stone stuck in place. Many stones in our walls were polished but have lost their sheen because of weathering. The best place to find genuine, sun-reflecting polish is on the surfaces of quartz veins and large crystals, since this mineral is chemically resistant enough to have kept its polish.

Glacial scratches on basalt traprock, central Massachusetts

Crescentic marks result from when one hard rock was pressed or whacked against another hard rock. As the name suggests, most have the shape of crescent moons, or the "smiles" on a golf ball, inch-scale fractures. They generally formed when a rounded quartzite boulder bounced along inside a meltwater stream just before it came to rest for good. Each smile-shaped, randomly oriented fracture records a hard bounce. Crescentic marks could also form when a hard boulder was pressed by the ice into bedrock. In this case the marks are not random but are instead aligned such that the tips of the curve point downglacier. If the pressure was high enough and if there was space, sometimes a crescent-shaped flake of stone was removed. If large enough, such flakes can end up as clam-shaped stones in a wall.

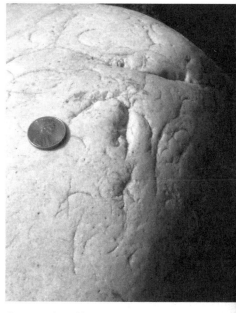

Crescent-shaped impact scars on a quartzite boulder, eastern Connecticut

Chattermark trails are rows of very small crescent marks nested into one another, usually the size of peas to pinheads, with the tips pointing in the direction of glacial movement. They formed where the rock was too hard to be striated, yet not quite hard enough to resist developing a row of cracks. Chattermarks indicate movement somewhat like the legs of a heavy table making small scuff marks when it is pulled across the floor. Each chattermark trail is the result of a dozen of more miniature ice quakes, seismic events that once rumbled through the ice.

Many people are under the mistaken impression that glacial stones are jagged, and stream-rolled ones are rounded. Actually, the base of an ice sheet rounds off corners, especially when the shear zone at the base of the ice is heavily loaded with sediment. In this zone, the movement is too slow for the stones to bounce. Instead, the corners of blocky stones are progressively crushed, or pecked apart by thousands of chance encounters with other stones. This process is self-reinforcing, as the more rounded a boulder becomes, the easier it is for it to roll across the land. This is why most glacial erratics and the largest granite boulders in a wall are usually somewhat rounded.

Cracked-egg stones have one side that is round (but not stream-polished), the other jagged and broken. They formed when a stone was being pecked into a smooth shape by the ice, then became caught up in a collision that broke the stone in half. These are also called half-rounded stones.

WEATHERING

The most primitive weathering mark is simply the stain or rind on the exterior of a stone. It can be of any color. Usually weathering marks on granite are gray, those

on basalt are rusty orange, those on sandstone a purple-black varnish, and those on dark mudrock are bleached.

Weathering also roughens a stone's exterior. This happens because the stone disintegrates from the outside in, mineral grain by mineral grain, each of which weathers at a different rate. Acidic rain baths can do the job alone, but the growth of lichens and frost action enhances the process as well. Large mineral grains produce coarse-textured surfaces, while small ones produce smooth surfaces.

The contour of many stones also is due to weathering. Each rock is a block of raw material being sculpted, one grain or fragment at a time, as nature whittles away the stone. The parts that are left sticking out tend to be the harder parts, usually veins or blobs of quartz or zones without mafic minerals. I call them standouts. Each shows us where the edge of the boulder used to be. But dugouts are just as common, places where the surface of the stone was locally excavated by weathering into pits or grooves. Standouts and dugouts show the amount of weathering that has

A zebra-striped pattern in silica-rich marble, Berkshires, Massachusetts

taken place since glaciation, since they wouldn't have survived glacial transport. What they tell us is that the shaping of stones is a constant, rather than an intermittent, process.

Mica-rich schists are often loaded with larger crystals. After the rock is split and weathered, the garnets produce a pebbled, bumpy pattern resembling reptile scales on an otherwise smooth surface, something like crocodile leather. In other cases, resistant veins inside the rock become manifest as ridges as the weaker host rock weathers away. When this happens to multiple veins that intersect, the pattern of ridges gives rise to a checkerboard appearance called box work. Finally, when a planar joint cuts through a rock consisting of thinly laminated strong and weak layers, the result after weathering is a surface that strongly resembles the grain of wood. When tightly folded, the rock can produce a column-shaped stone that mirrors the shape of a log, sometimes complete with knots. On more than a few occasions, I have pulled stones from a wall, thinking they were blocks of petrified wood or old cedar fence posts. Instead, they were pseudo-petrified wood stones.

Boulders and cobbles of quartzite, especially when very smooth, are often completely unweathered, lichen-free, and polished. They sit like sentinels through century after century, as if completely impervious to the weather. They practically are. Most other rocks, however, are slowly disintegrating as they sit in stone walls.

Weathered surfaces can be used to determine if stones have been removed, added, rebuilt, or flipped around. Weathering acts differently on the top, bottom, and outside faces of a stone. The exposed top is usually tarnished, lichen-covered, and weathered roughly, with the low spots corresponding to places where rain collects and lasts longer, so it has more time to dissolve the stone. The exposed edge (or edges, in the case of a corner) usually exhibits a grain like that of weather-beaten driftwood, with the foliations (rather than the growth rings) etched in. Conversely, the bottom and inside faces of stones buried inside the wall are much fresher and lichen-free. Undersides of stones sometimes collect precipitates of lime and iron. Being able to tell the top, outside, inside, and bottom side of stones allows the stone-wall detective to decide whether a wall has been rebuilt, whether stones have been pilfered, and whether new stones have been added to an old wall.

TOOL MARKS

Drill holes in marble at a quarry, southern Vermont

Humans modify stones using many of the same techniques the ice sheet did—grinding, polishing, scratching, inscribing, and breaking. You might encounter all kinds of man-made marks on stones in walls, even the occasional engraving. Sometimes engraved stones end up in walls because cemeteries were abandoned, or because the engravers made a mistake, so the stone was tossed out as waste. One thing is certain: No farmer in his or her right mind would engrave fieldstone before setting it into a wall.

The most common tool marks found in stone walls are the remains of drill holes adorning the face of quarried stones. They tend to be cigar-sized, half-cylinder holes, several inches long and spaced anywhere from four inches to two feet apart. If the holes are slightly irregular in shape and of different depth, they usually indicate use of a star drill (also called a star chisel), which was hammered into the rock, pulverizing the crystals with repeated hammer blows. The star drill was something like a jackhammer without the jack, or the pneumatic assistance. Its familiar mark is diagnostic of hand-quarried stone taken prior to the late nineteenth century. A rock with intact drill holes was one that refused to break.

The star-drill technique was simple enough to have been used by individual farmers, usually only to cut specialized stone for sills and foundations. To a lesser extent, star drills were used to

Hand-carved engraving on a tombstone, Concord, Massachusetts

break up residual stones that blemished otherwise nearly perfect fields. A star-drill hole on a rounded boulder inside a wall almost always represents the final clearing of a field on a farm of considerable wealth.

More recent developments included the jackhammer (which is really a chisel) and the steam drill. If the edge of a stone bears evidence of

Ancient (colonial era) quarry marks on granite, southern New Hampshire

thousands of chisel marks, a jackhammer or some kind of mechanical chisel was probably used. If the drill holes are smoother and more uniform in shape than star-drilled holes, especially if they have slight ridges around the hole, they were probably made using a steam drill. Coal- and wood-fired steam power was converted to mechanical power used to turn a rod attached to a hardened drill bit. This cut out a core of stone large enough to receive a charge of dynamite, which was then used to blast the stone apart. Though more expensive, steam drilling was used extensively in quarries or on estates where the amount of stonework justified the cost.

Later technologies have skipped the drilling of holes entirely, cutting the stone instead with saws, which leave telltale clues on the flat surfaces of stones. Prior to the Civil War, saw marks were generally found only on soft rocks, principally soapstone, marble, and various grades of sandstone. Originally, rocks were cut with hardened-steel hand saws, which left ribs or corrugations. More recently,

Polish (dark) and pecking (light) on a granite tombstone, central Massachusetts

Weathered rind scratched away by construction equipment, eastern Connecticut

rocks of all hardness have been cut with wire line saws impregnated with diamond or carbide grit. Many saw-cut surfaces are then polished, to remove surface irregularities and to produce a high gloss.

The latest technology is to use a jet, which is like a miniature, highly focused blowtorch into which micro bursts of water are pulsed. No rock can withstand the violent alternation of extreme heat and rapid quenching. These jets cut slowly through rock as if it were butter.

More common than even drilled or cut stones are those that were whacked into shape by nothing more than the blows of a hammer. These are particularly common in laid and chinked walls, where the stones were fitted carefully. Sometimes the hammer-blow mark is little more than a fracture that is fresher than the typical weathered surface of the stone. More rarely, the protruding tip of a stone was crushed by striking it inward, essentially pecking it into shape. Typically, shaped stones are not present on fieldstone fence-line walls, but are diagnostic of carefully built walls nearer the center of farms and villages.

Scrape marks are becoming much more common on stones. When a large stone is encountered during excavations, it must be pushed about by the blade of a bulldozer or lifted into the scoop of a loader/backhoe. Invariably, this leaves streaks of light-colored crushed rock. After the crushing has washed away, however, the shallow scrapes and broad grooves remain. Usually these scrape marks penetrate all the way through the patina on the stone, leaving permanent clues to recent rough handling. Scrape marks were far less common in colonial and early America. Their presence usually indicates a wall dating no further back than about the 1930s, the era when petroleum-powered bulldozers, loaders, and backhoes became common.

PART II

A CLOSER LOOK AT WALLS

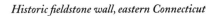
Historic fieldstone wall, eastern Connecticut

CHAPTER 5

WALL SIZE AND SHAPE

Dunes, caves, canyons, floodplains, ledges, and beaches—we consider them familiar landforms because they are natural features of the landscape. We consider canals, millponds, and seawalls architecture because they are part of the built environment. The somewhat arbitrary distinction between landform and architecture works fine for modern stone walls in cities and towns, where human-built structures are dominant and where people still live. But the dichotomy fades almost completely when we consider crude stone walls tumbling apart in the forest. In such settings, the natural presence is dominant, even though an earlier human presence is undeniable. In a sense, such stone walls are no less wild than the trees rooted in their basal stones, or the wild turkeys that dwell nearby. Under these circumstances, it's best to treat them as landforms as well.

Walls are not wholly unlike the ledges from which they were born. In fact, one could argue that stone walls are little more than second-generation ledges; their building blocks were torn from parent ledges by ice some twenty thousand years ago

A natural ledge resembling a well-laid wall, southern New Hampshire

before being reassembled by humans fifteen thousand years later into longer, straighter versions of the ancestral form. In particularly well-built but unchinked walls, the cracks between flat stones in a wall resemble those of the original fractured ledge.

Stone walls are most often observed from the side, as if they were the branchless trunks of exceptionally long, fallen trees. Every wall has some height above the ground, and some length along it. The breadth of a wall, or its thickness, is apparent only when we look down from above. I consider a stone wall to be any continuous row of large stones or stack of smaller ones that is more than four times as long as it is wide. Anything shorter is a cluster or pile of stones, not a wall.

WALL DIMENSIONS

The length of a wall is measured parallel to the ground, usually ignoring gaps where stones have been knocked down or where the rocks have been pirated for other purposes. Freestanding walls that are longer than a typical barn (about 150 feet), regardless of their form or structure, almost always mark former fence lines that once divided patches of land; many were also parallel to roads. Shorter walls, especially those that are higher on one side, were usually related to some kind of construction activity associated with buildings, dams, and bridges.

When a wall is carefully laid and capped with flat stones, its height is usually quite uniform. Height is uneven for poorly built walls with an odd mix of stones, especially if they have sunk, sprawled, and toppled here and there. In this circumstance, the height of a wall is best characterized by its average rather than by its minimum or maximum height.

The vast majority of stone walls are thigh-high. This is not coincidental—it corresponds to the height at which humans are optimally strong. In many cases,

A high seawall below the Cliff Walk in Newport, Rhode Island

it wasn't worth the trouble to lift heavy stones much higher. Other walls range from knee-high to waist-high, but very few approach shoulder height.

There is much confusion between a stone wall and a stone fence. Regardless of material, walls are upright structures serving to enclose, divide, support, or protect. The principal connotation is structural. In contrast, fences prevent entry or egress, and the principal connotation is functional. Stone structures more than chest height (3.5 to 4.5 feet), especially if they are long and continuous, are usually considered to be fences. Short segments of any height—for example, a retaining wall—are usually not considered fences because they were not built to control access either into or out of a piece of land.

A freestanding single wall, Block Island, Rhode Island

Normally, the term *wall* is used when the typical structures are massive, low, and made of slabby stone. The term *fence* is used when the structure is a single stack that meets or exceeds chest height. To prevent further confusion, I recommend that we consider stone fences to be those that are both freestanding and roughly chest height to an average person (3.5 to 4.5 feet high, which was the minimum legal height of a fence during colonial times). I suspect that only one wall segment in a thousand is tall enough to enclose a flock of sheep without the aid of wire or wood. Fewer still are too tall to see over.

Even below the fence vs. nonfence distinction, there is still a strong relationship between the height of a stone wall and its original purpose. Walls that are ankle-high usually indicate little more than the early accumulation of stone below a former fence. Knee-high walls may have fallen from former glory, but most were never more than sprawling heaps resulting from more prolonged accumulation of stone at the edges of fields, whether dumped in loads or stacked one stone at a time. Thigh-high walls are typical because a boundary marker must be that tall to stand above the grass. Waist-high walls usually indicate places where rolled boulders have been evened off with extra stone.

A rectangular stack, coastal Maine

The width of a wall is more variable than its height. For well-built, quarry-capped boundary and estate walls, the top is usually the best place to measure width. However, that's the worst place to measure the width of crudely built walls, because width at the top is nothing more than the diameter of the top row of stones. For all walls, the width at the base almost always exceeds the width at the top, partly because a wider base is required for structural support, but also because walls sprawl with age, as they settle or erode.

Many low walls, especially long heaps of stone along the edges of a former field, have highly variable widths. The thick sections almost always represent intermittent dumping of stone, whether rolled off a stone boat (a stout wooden sled built to haul stone and pulled by livestock) or tipped from a cart. The thin sections represent stone merely tossed along the base of a fence.

"Single" walls are little more than a row of stones stacked one above the other—primarily to fence in a pasture, and to a lesser extent to clear the land of stone. Single walls are only as wide as the diameter of the largest stones used at the base.

"Double" walls are two or more rows wide, and built from both sides rather than simply stacked up like cordwood. They are more common, and serve many purposes beyond that of fencing, such as stone disposal, boundary marking, and aesthetic enhancement.

Some double walls are truly colossal, as much as five feet high and more than twenty feet wide. Like the famous walls of the ancient world, these represent places where vast quantities of waste stone were disposed of, regardless of how tidy the resulting pile. Normally this was done as a single project by either a work crew or a community-wide effort. It could also be done where smaller, stone-rimmed fields were converted into larger ones, or where a fallow pasture was upgraded, often to a tillage field.

Some low double walls are well built and have holes or identations along the top spaced eight to twelve feet apart. These holes were places where wooden posts were inserted to create a compound fence—wood on the top, stone on the bottom. More often, poles were mounted above the stone with supporting A-frames.

A classic inward-slanted, battered, well-laid double wall, eastern Connecticut

The stage to which a property was developed can be read from its walls. Thin rows and heaps may outline the trace of wooden fences that have long since rotted away. Either the fence had demarcated a recently developed pasture or the property never evolved past the "pioneering farm" stage. Single walls, especially if high, suggest more prolonged use and, in rare cases, a shortage of wood for fencing.

Double walls suggest that the builder-farmer had enough stone and enough leisure time to create lasting boundary walls. Extra-wide walls with a regular face and fairly straight sides indicate a short-lived but intensive effort at land clearing, often the conversion of a stony pasture to a tillage or mowing field. To build such a wall requires the wealth and free time for capital improvement, which suggests a property having become an established farm.

An extra-wide disposal wall for clearing a field, southern New Hampshire

SHAPE

If you could look at the cross-section of an intact stone wall, you would see variation in the wall's shape. Many walls have a crude triangular geometry in cross section—one stone wide at the top and several stones wide at the base. Such walls have definite sides (also called faces), but no top. Usually these triangular walls are built of rounded cobbles and boulders, which, unless mortared, simply cannot be arranged into a wall with flat sides. They are triangular by default.

When stones have a dominantly spherical shape, it is physically impossible to fit them together well. This leaves plenty of pore spaces, especially along the top tier or two. From the side, there is often so much pore space that the walls resemble lace; hence the vernacular term "lace wall." Found from Nantucket to Long Island, and occasionally along the Rhode Island shore, lace walls are usually interpreted as places where early colonial sheep ranching was common, the argument being that the sheep would not breach a lace wall because they were fearful of its collapse. Though this must be part of the explanation, the presence of lace walls where sheep were not ranched—and their absence in places where sheep were common—suggest that lace walls were principally the result of building tall, triangular panels with rounded melon-sized stones.

An extremely rounded or cannonball wall has sloping sides. At the other end of the extreme, a perfect vertical-sided wall would be built of either interlocking stones, or, more likely, flat, book-shaped stones. Between these extremes, the degree to which a drystone (mortar-free) wall tapers upward is highly related to the jaggedness of the typical stone surface, and the proportion of rounded, or semi-rounded, stones it contains.

Triangular form commonly used for fieldstone fences, eastern Rhode Island

Walls taller than knee-high, especially if made of flat stones, usually have clearly defined tops and sides. Such walls usually take the form of trapezoids in cross-section because the base is wider than the top. To a stonemason, the narrowing of the wall upward is called battering. Most walls built by masons are carefully battered to a uniform angle, ranging from about one part in five to one part in twelve.

The presence of well-defined tops and battered sides on a wall is an important clue; regardless of present setting or condition, it signals a deliberate construction project by a person with some skill, who gave serious attention to stone selection and placement. Such a wall indicates prosperity or wealth, often both. It is when such well-built walls stand intact in the deepest woods that we find the strongest juxtaposition between civilization and wildness.

Stone pillar of a former bridge, southern Vermont

SYMMETRY

Many freestanding walls look the same on both sides; they are said to be symmetrical in cross-section. In stonemason language, they have identical faces. But even more walls look different on opposite sides; they are asymmetrical. Like size and shape, the presence or absence of symmetry is one of the most vital clues for

A square-topped vertical-sided, tightly laid estate wall, Newport, Rhode Island

A symmetrical double wall with an unusual facade, eastern Connecticut

interpreting stone walls; it speaks of the patterns of land use on both sides, whether similar or contrasting.

Many walls have one or more conspicuous asymmetries. For example, freestanding walls are often more carefully built on the side that faces the house, because that is the direction from which they are most commonly seen. (When one side is well built and the other rather formless, the wall is said to have a front face and a back face.) Similarly, the end view of a wall crossed by a road or driveway is likely to be more massive and better built because that is where the extra strength for a gate or barway (see p. 79) was needed. If a wall is formless on the outside but contains a careful structure on the inside, it has tumbled apart from the outside in. Conversely, a wall with a mortar-free face and a mortared interior is a false drystone wall, which can be dangerous because it may collapse suddenly without warning.

An asymmetrical retaining wall with one face, southern New Hampshire

CHAPTER 6

STRUCTURE AND STYLE

Beauty is often about finding the right balance between order and chaos.

Stone walls help us find that balance, whether by framing hillside pastures or by making a straight line through the otherwise disorganized environment of the woods, where daubs of color and texture from shrubs, stumps, brush, hollows, stranded boulders, animal marks, and patches of ferns are the rule. Even if we consider only the stones, the most aesthetically appealing stone walls are often those with a perfect tension between the disorder of odd-shaped, odd-colored, odd-sized fieldstones and the order associated either with regular blocks of quarrystone or with the regular lines of the wall. In both cases, the wall adds a rigid, classical beauty to the more impulsive, romantic charm of odd stones and the weedy growth of nature. To just barely contain the disorder seems to me an ideal compromise with nature. We tame it, but leave it largely free.

Walls also bring psychological order to the everyday complexity of human life. As boundary markers, they announce a claim to land. As fences, they offer strength against unwanted human intrusion and the tempests of nature. As architecture, they add coherence to what would otherwise be rubble, announcing a personal, local, seemingly permanent human mark on the world.

The architecture of a wall—

A triangular segment of facing wall for a barn ramp, eastern Connecticut

the way the stones are put together in rows, lines, and tiers—dictates whether it will stand for centuries, or fall apart after the first spring thaw. There is a palpable relationship between wall structure and wall shape. The more regular the shape of the stones, and the more order invested in arranging them, the taller and straighter is the wall, and the longer it will last. A wall built of odd-shaped stones usually dribbles along through the woods. A high, sturdy wall usually has slabby flat stones stacked close together. The wall's form must follow the lead of its material.

ORDER

Every wall that's more than a dump of stone is a piece of folk art, reflecting the idiosyncratic, artistic impulse of its builder. The presence of art is signaled by any nonrandom, nonstructural arrangements of the stones into some sort of a pattern, perhaps an alternate arrangement of large and small stones, the selective placement of light-colored stones, the spaced punctuation of an upright stone in otherwise flat courses—anything that departs from the laying of the stones as if they were bricks or logs. The artistic order within a wall is easily seen, though impossible to measure.

Levels of order: dumped (left), stacked (center), and laid (right), eastern Connecticut

The possibilities of expressing oneself with stone are endless. For example, the builder may have inserted white quartz boulders or square granite blocks at regular intervals along the line of the wall. He may have set two large slabs to form the letter T, or one long one and two short ones to make a cross. Pebbles can be arranged into a circle. Individual masons often have their own signature style. Local guilds of masons may have their own traditions—for example, the Narragansett style of "Indian" walls consists of an arrangment of square blocky stones arranged in a mosaic, almost like a plaid.

The material order within a wall is largely determined by the degree to which the stones are fitted together. A wall that is well fitted has very little void space; it signals human deliberateness and plenty of available time, since the smaller stones had to be either selected or shaped to fit progressively into smaller leftover holes. Stacking a set of regular-shaped stones takes much more time than merely heaping them. Stacking a mixture of different stone sizes and shapes takes even more time.

The degree to which stone is fitted together—its packing—is an important diagnostic tool for interpreting why a wall was built. A dumped wall, the most disordered state, is where stones have been merely rolled, tossed, or dropped against a fence line—individually or in groups—with no order invested in their arrangement. Usually the width and height of the wall vary randomly. This degree of order is most commonly associated with low height, irregular form, and rounded stones. Such "walls" meet the definition of a wall only because the stone collection creates a continuous pile. They indicate the most primitive stage of construction, and are usually located along the edges of remote pastures.

An artistic ordering of stone, Newport, Rhode Island

Next in sequence is the stacked wall, also known as a "tossed," "farmer's," "thrown," or "pasture" wall. In a stacked wall, the stones are placed one above the other with no concern for the fit of the stones beyond nesting them together, as if they were logs in a stack of firewood. There is some order to the arrangement, but not very much. Horizontal layers of stone, if present, might be accidental. Stacking is the best means for getting stones out of the way, even when making a wall

A dumped wall at the side of a field, eastern Connecticut

Recently laid wall in the foreground with older stacked wall behind it, eastern Connecticut

wasn't the main purpose. If the goal was also to make a wall, then stacking is the most efficient way of creating an upright structure to mark a boundary or make a fence. Both purposes—clearing and marking or fencing—were inseparably merged in the vast majority of New England stone walls. But because most stone was moved the shortest possible distance (to the edge of the field), and because many enclosures lack stone on two or more sides, the disposal of stone was probably the most common rationale for stacking, rather than dumping or carefully fitting, stones.

A placed wall is slightly more ordered than a dumped wall, but less so than a stacked wall. This type of order consists of a line of boulders or slabs that were rolled, skidded, dropped, or levered into place such that they touch each other. If smaller stones are stacked or laid above the line of large stones, then the degree of order changes from placed to a stacked or laid wall instead, respectively.

In a laid wall, the stones are placed with some degree of care beyond mere stacking. Things to look for in a laid wall include well-defined layers of stone, a deliberate arrangement of one stone above two and two above one, and placements of large stones across walls and corners. Laid walls are most common in areas where the rocks are highly concen-

trated, have the shape of slabs, and are generally one- and two-handers. Laid walls are most
common as well-built double walls on established farms and as retaining walls in village
and now suburban settings, where most new
walls are laid walls. Usually there were two ob-
jectives in mind for laying a wall, rather than
merely stacking it: enhancing structural stability and creating a thing of beauty. The builder
of a laid wall has crossed the threshold away
from the clearing and storage of stone to the
use of stone as an architectural material. Laid
walls also convey a sense of pride, property, and
status.

Triangular stones carefully laid, then chinked, western Massachusetts

A chinked wall exhibits the maximum degree
of packing. In this type, smaller stones—many
prepared with the blow of a mason's hammer—
are fitted into the gaps between large stones to produce an even face, with hardly
any gaps between the stones. Chinking does not add to the structural strength of
the wall, since the stones usually don't support any weight; unless mortared, most
can be pulled from the wall with finger and thumb. Hence, chinking is always about
art. It signifies that another cultural threshold has been crossed, one beyond structural stability and the classic folk-art simplicity of the New England wall.

Each step on the ladder from disorder to order—dump, stack, place, lay,
chink—signals a shift in the intentions of its builders. For dumped walls, the focus
was on simply clearing the field. Ironically, such walls are probably more visible
now that they lie beneath the shade of the forest canopy then when they accumulated along fence lines, where brush and vines must have obscured them. Stacked
walls mark a turning point as the focus shifted away from the field toward the
fence. Laid walls are always about the wall as either a strong barrier or a prideful
territorial marker, usually both. Chinked walls are always about the art.

Based on my experience, and discounting the damage done to wild walls over
decades and centuries, I suspect that the vast majority of New England walls are
crude stacks. By using this degree of order, farmers were able to manage stone refuse while simultaneously marking boundaries and making fences, or at least the

Three courses of granite boulders, Poland Spring, Maine

bottom halves of fences. The concentration of more highly ordered walls—laid and chinked—around centers of wealth and influence, and their absence in much of the backcountry, makes a powerful statement about the motives of the early American farmer, who was too busy helping to build a nation to fuss with the artistic arrangement of stone.

PLACEMENT

There is much more to the architecture of a wall than merely the degree to which it is fitted. There is also the arrangement of stones relative to each other within the wall. The simplest way of arranging stones is to place them side by side in a single horizontal layer, or course, of stone. The most familiar course is a single layer of bricks (artificial stone) in a standard brick wall. Courses are present but harder to define in fieldstone walls because the shapes are more irregular, unless they are capped with a course of flat or decorative capstones.

One or more courses of stone are arranged into tiers or levels. The simplest stone wall consists of a single line of boulders, rolled or skidded off the field, then abutted against each other. Such a wall has not only a single course but a single tier as well. Next in complexity, and much more common, is a typical fieldstone pasture wall, which consists of multiple courses arranged into a single tier; such walls look similar from base to top. Almost as common, however, are three-tiered fieldstone boundary walls, which have:

- a basal tier composed of large foundation stones
- a main tier consisting of multiple courses of standard fieldstones
- and a top tier of large flat stones.

The presence of tiers would seem to suggest deliberate planning. This need not be the case; the builder may have used different sizes and shapes in different levels because the supply of stone changed during upward construction of the wall.

Within most tiers, the courses are usually even, or uniform. However, they can also be graded—successive courses changing gradually,

Two tiers: a wall built on a wall, Newport, Rhode Island

usually from large stones at the bottom to smaller stones upward. Alternatively, the builder may have chosen to set down a course of flat stones, followed by a course of round stones, or a course of large stones. Courses of large and small stones, or flat and round ones, can alternate within a single tier.

There are two common specialty tiers. A foundation tier, whether made of gravel, boulders, or well-fitted stones, is widely distributed across New England, though present only in the best-built walls. The most common top tier for a fieldstone wall, especially a wall built from both sides, is to finish it off with a layer of capstones, which are larger, flatter, and more evenly shaped than those making up the bulk of the wall. Such walls are said to have a "hard" cap, because the capstones usually span both sides of a double wall. When capstones are absent, there is often a layer of rubble or smaller stones in the middle. These are said to have a "puddle" cap.

Sometimes the capstones were simply the best-shaped fieldstones culled from the available

A wall in eastern Connecticut showing how stone size is usually graded from large (bottom) to small (top).

A gravel-filled trench for the foundation of a future quarrystone wall, eastern Connecticut

supply and reserved for the final course. In many cases, however, especially on early-twentieth-century estates, early fieldstone walls were rebuilt and finished off with a hard cap of stone imported from a quarry. The presence of capstones in general, and quarried capstones in particular, proves that some element of planning for aesthetic appeal went into construction of the wall.

A special variant of stone wall is most common in colonial, thoroughly English, fairly wealthy, usually Anglican settlements, such as those surrounding Narragansett Bay, Rhode Island. At Little Compton, for example, fieldstone walls are finished off with a top tier of stones laid not flat but on edge, across the wall. Stones arranged in such a way are called copestones; they expose their jagged, pointed edges and tips upward. In many cases the stones were actually broken to form spikes, which were then mortared into the top of the wall pointing skyward, as if they were iron spikes. Intimidation, rather than strength, is the message they convey on no-trespassing walls.

When discussing the width of a wall, I introduced the idea of single versus double walls, shorthand for sin-

Copestones cemented into a wall, Rhode Island

gle-line and double-line walls. Lines are to a wall's footprint on the land as courses are to its side view. Well-built double walls actually have three lines. The most regular face of each stone was placed on the outside, with the smaller pointed, misshapen faces on the inside. To hold the stones in place, the center was usually filled with a line of rubble. A hard-capped double wall has only one line on top.

Well-built double walls, complete with a rubble fill and capstones, are often referred to as estate walls. Building more than fifty feet of such a wall was an expensive capital improvement requiring more financing than even well-established farmers could afford. Hence, the wealth manifest in estate walls came generally from industry, rather than agriculture. Most estate walls were built by hired labor under the supervision of architects. The actual hands that lifted the stones were most often immigrants working in gangs.

Many walls are a hybrid of single and double walls. They may be bouldery and double at the base, then topped with a panel of stones using a

A single wall widened at its tip for a barway, southern Vermont

single-wall technique, often to the height of a fence. The large boulders represent an early stage in the farm clearing; the stable stack of stones above them represents stone that was unearthed later during the tilling and pasturing of the soil.

Triple walls are extra-wide, and their purpose was usually disposal. Two stacks of stone, spaced as much as twenty feet apart, are filled with all manner of stones developed when a new line of stones was built up against a preexisting double wall. I have seen this in many twentieth-century orchards, after the conversion of old wall-rimmed fields; stone was hauled outward from newly planted fruit trees, then heaped against a preexisting wall.

Almost all abandoned walls have flanking aprons composed of fallen stones, soil, and sediment that have accumulated after construction. Such aprons are nestled into the corner formed by soil and wall. The presence of a well-developed apron indicates some antiquity to a wall; it means there has been enough time to accumulate the wedge of sediment and fallen stones, probably a half century or more.

The lexicon of drystone masonry is full of terms for stones used for special purposes, some of which are occasionally seen in fieldstone walls. Most enigmatic are thrufters, which generally are blade-shaped stones large enough to span the gap from one face of the wall to another, thereby helping to bind them together (like a cross-brace). In other words, they occupy both faces at once. Wedge-shaped stones are often used to level thrufters.

MORTAR AND MATRIX

By definition, stone walls are composed of stone. But the void spaces between the stones, both inside and out, are always filled with something else, be it rubble, cement, organic material, air, and even water.

The proportion of void space varies greatly. At one extreme, perfectly brick-shaped blocks can be laid carefully end-to-end, yielding no more than a percent or two void space by volume. At the other extreme are the melon-shaped boulders that, even when perfectly stacked, yield a void space of 26 percent. Chunky stones with odd points and angles lead to a lace wall, some seeming to be more air than stone. It has been argued that the excess space was a way of "stretching" the supply of stone to make taller fences. Some even argue that lace walls were built to keep the wind from blowing them over. Who knows? Though lace walls look as if they could

Culture: mason's tools for a modern project, eastern Connecticut

collapse at any moment, many have stood for a century.

A wall's matrix is any solid material, as opposed to air or water, that fills the void between stones. Walls lacking a mortar matrix are called drystone walls. When mortar is present we refer to it as a mortared wall, colloquially known as a "wet" wall. Such mortar is usually composed of Portland cement, which came into popular use only after the Civil War. Traditional lime mortar is making a comeback, if only for authenticity's sake.

The presence or absence of mortar provides several easy-to-use clues to the origin and significance of stone walls. First, nobody would bother to mortar stones if the wall was being erected as a linear landfill to hold waste stone. Any wall with mortar must have had some architectural purpose. Second, the presence of cement mortar in a wall usually indicates a twentieth-century construction, though its absence signifies nothing, as the traditional practice of building drystone walls wasn't given up when cement was invented. Stone-wall purists, who consider stone-masonry as a contest between human skill and gravity, see the gluing of stones together with cement as a form of cheating.

Mortar dissolved away from cobbles, central Vermont

The simple distinction between dry and wet walls is not without its problems. First, mortar was seldom used to fill all of the void space. Most commonly, it was applied only to the top tier of stones to help bond them together and to prevent their theft, especially when large capstones were not available. Mortar was also sometimes applied only to the face of the wall to bind its outermost stones. This has been a common practice in urban retaining walls, especially those built of cobbles and small boulders. Also common was filling the interior voids with cement, into which the outer stones were pressed before it hardened. This approach was used when a drystone wall might have been preferred, but there wasn't the time, labor, or skill to do it right.

Drystone walls are often patched with mortar as a temporary fix. Such patch jobs don't last for long because they address only the symptom of ongoing failure, not its cause. As patches of cement are added one at a time, they darken to different shades, creating a sorry sight.

All mortared walls are disasters waiting to happen. Mortaring the stones creates a rigid block that (unlike reinforced concrete) is never strong enough to withstand the heaving and swelling of the soil, whether from moisture or from tree roots. The second problem is that cement is essentially a lime-based artificial mineral, sworn enemy to the acidity of New England's rains (4.5–5.0 pH) and to its soil moisture. But even if rainwater were distilled to neutrality, the lime would still react with the common silicate minerals to produce acidic clay and dust.

When a mortared wall is first built, the stones are actually held together by the "gluing" effect of the cement, a particle-to-particle cohesion. Within a few years, however, the chemical reaction produces a gap between stone and cement. Once the gluing effect is gone, what holds the wall together is not cohesion but the three-dimensional framework shape of the mortar, which "cups" the stones in place in the same way that an egg carton holds eggs, giving them no place to tumble. When such walls fail, however, which they eventually do, there is no warning, no gradual shifting of the stones. Usually they go all at once, sometimes dangerously.

Mortar broken free to become a stone, Rhode Island

A good example of such a failure was evident on the wall surrounding the sunken garden at Hill-Stead Museum in Farmington, Connecticut, the site of an important New England summer poetry festival. The wall was later skillfully patched.

The eventual demise of a once-mortared wall, followed by its skillful rebuilding into a drystone wall, produces a wall with one of the most interesting histories. The original mortar, having disintegrated, creates a population of artificial stones made of cement that are stacked into the rebuilt wall. Such a wall is a victory monument to traditional drystone building practices because it is built, in part, of the remains of a failed mortared wall.

Though drystone walls were originally built

with nothing but air in the void spaces, many are no longer dry. Thousands of walls have become submerged beneath water when the shores of lakes and swamps were raised for water-supply projects and flood-control reservoirs. The most famous are the many villages submerged between 1939 and 1946 to form Quabbin Reservoir, the chief public water supply for the city of Boston. Clearly, these are very wet so-called drystone walls.

Many abandoned walls in the woods aren't dry either, except for their top stones. Much of the volume in such walls is filled with moist organic material—soil, leaves, twigs, roots, humus, and rhizomes. This is especially true when one or more of a wall's aprons reaches more than halfway to the summit, either because of sedimentation on the side or because the wall has subsided into the soil. However, even a wall that hasn't subsided or been flanked by sediment on one side can become in-filled with organic matter. This happens most often when vines cover the face of a wall and the roots work their way inward, creating mulch.

The matrix of many walls, especially near the ground, becomes filled with mineral soil. Streams deposit sediment there. Soil creeping along the slope infiltrates the pores. Sometimes the sheer weight of a wall drives it into the soft soil, as if it were a wedge; this happens because the pore spaces caused by roots, animal activity, wetting and drying, and freezing and thawing are more likely to close beneath the weight of a wall than to remain open.

Basically, over time, the matrix of even the best-built walls becomes filled with what resembles potting soil. This mulch leads to the growth of woody vegetation, which pries tiers, courses, lines, and chinking apart over time.

CHAPTER 7

LAYOUT AND PURPOSE

All stone walls are made of one or more segments. A wall segment is any continuous part along the line of the wall in which the arrangement and composition of the stones are similar, or vary consistently. For example, a single-line segment may widen into an uncapped double-line segment, then into a capped one, all as part of the same wall. Segments typically range from fifty to several hundred feet long. They merge to form continuous walls, which can merge to form enclosures (or partial enclosures), which can cluster to form farmsteads and villages. In biology, the cell is the fundamental unit; in stone wall science, the segment is.

The trace of a segment is its geometric footprint on the land. A straight trace is most common because property division almost always used straight lines, producing squares, triangles, or odd-shaped polygons. A curved trace usually indicates a natural boundary of some sort, with the curve following the contour of the land or a geological transition. The gapped trace is found where walls were poorly built, have been poached for their stone, or have been knocked over by falling trees. Zigzag traces, though rare, are low walls that accumulated piecemeal beneath a Virginia rail fence (aka the zigzag or worm fence).

Walls end in one of three basic ways. Some just dribble into nothing (dribble ends). These signify a primitive state of construction, usually

One wall with two segments defined by stone size, central New Hampshire

because the wall ended as the supply of stone gave out nearby. Just as often, however, an end is well built, its stone arranged for extra strength. Built ends usually signify some sort of gate or a decorative touch. The end of a segment may be buttressed with a post, pillar, or boulder; anything that keeps the stones from cascading forward parallel to the line of the wall.

Three visible segments of straight traces, which are the most common, eastern Connecticut

Although segments are usually similar in form along their length, most stacked walls and virtually all laid walls contain one or more special culturally mandated structures. Crossings, either special gaps in the wall or the means to climb over the wall, are most common. The most common crossings are barways, which are gaps between segments, typically ten to fifteen feet wide, usually with crudely built ends. Barways are the remains of primitive gates made of wooden "bars," whether rails or poles, that were inserted into gaps between the built ends of the walls. Barways may be elaborate or so plain as to be virtually unnoticed. The weirdest barway I ever saw was a short length of electric wire fence fronting a tall wall, essentially an electric bar. Gates are similar to barways but are usually narrower and better built, often with a post for holding the gate. Most often they were built for pedestrian access, being too narrow for a vehicle. Iron gates were often set into posts; rusted remnants of many gates are present in stone posts. Of course, gates and barways merge into one another, the only difference being their width.

Stiles are places for humans to get over and through walls without the presence of bars or gates. A very narrow gap, especially if it is well built and too small for a gate, is called an open stile. These were built to provide human access and egress through the wall of an enclosed space (field or yard) but prevent movement of livestock, usually cattle and horses. Sometimes they are nothing more than a slot between two boulders. The step stile is a pedestrian stairway over a wall, the number of steps determined by the height of the wall. These are usually made of tabular or blade-shaped stones strong enough to support a human, with one end embedded in the stone wall and the other projecting outward as a step. A bridge stile, a wedge-shaped mass of stone or dirt on each side so a person can walk up and over, is very rare.

Several other types of ends are less aesthetic. A pinhead refers to the widening of a wall segment at its open end. If well built, the pinhead suggests the intentional strengthening of the end for a barway or gate. If merely a wider pile or stack of stones, the pinhead suggests that stones were being disposed of from a vehicle on a cartway or lane; sometimes the pile has even grown to bury the original end. Related to a pinhead is a flap—an opening in a formerly continuous wall where the stones were simply pushed or moved out of the way to create a road or trail. Flaps usually come in pairs, both ends pointing toward the direction in which the wall was pushed open. Two long flaps suggest that the gap was bulldozed into existence.

Curved trace in an ornate wall, Newport, Rhode Island

Dribble tip, where stones disappear gradually, eastern Connecticut

JUNCTIONS

Segments join each other at junctions. Two features of junctions are important. First is the way in which the stones fit together. In woven junctions the stones overlap one another, indicating that the segments were built simultaneously. Sometimes these are called seamless junctions. In abutting junctions, the stones of the younger segment are built flush against those of the older. Second is the way their traces fit together. In corner junctions there is an abrupt angle (usually 90 degrees) between the traces. Corner junctions are named for the number of corners they contain: L-junctions have one corner; T-junctions have two; X-junctions have four; Y-junctions occur where three walls come together from different directions. In-line junctions occur where the segments join along the line of the wall.

From the perspective of the field or pasture, the number of consecutive corner junctions—either clockwise or counterclockwise—determines the degree of enclosure. For a four-sided field, one corner creates a half-enclosure, assuming both walls span the length of their respective sides. Two corners create a three-quarter enclosure. Complete enclosure is next because the third corner requires the fourth.

A gate hung on a post abutting a reinforced end, western Massachusetts

End of segment buttressed by a boulder, eastern Connecticut

Built ends, which add strength and decoration, eastern Connecticut

DETERMINING A WALL'S PURPOSE

The epicenter of cultural space on farmsteads was the barn, whose foundation walls and stone pens are often still present. In one direction, often upwind from the barn, are the cellar holes and garden walls of the house. In the other direction, often downwind from the barn, are stockyard walls, those that once surrounded tillage fields and pastures; then, finally, come outer boundary walls.

Pinheads, which occur where extra stones are dumped at an end, Acadia, Maine

All of these walls were built for one or more purposes. Since form follows function, we can usually interpret past functions from the present form, even though many walls met several purposes simultaneously.

Except for deliberate construction projects near the barn and house, almost all stone walls started out as places to dispose of stone—essentially linear landfills, elongate collections of stone refuse. The key diagnostic element for a disposal wall is disorder; it is either a sprawling dumped pile or a broad stack.

Walls were also built to provide structural support. Some are the foundations of what were once buildings. Most of these are generally low to the ground, have flat, even tops, and contain large slabby stones at the corners. Those around barns usually have very large stones, especially near the top, and the

Stone culled from a pile, used to create laid double walls, eastern Connecticut

large stones are carefully leveled with wedge-shaped stones. Many outbuildings, sheds, and haystacks had small foundation walls as well. These are often flimsy, low, one- to three-sided enclosures, usually in settings detached from the center of the farmstead. The clue to identifying walls built for foundation are their flat, even tops and massive corners.

Retaining walls were built not to support a building but to stabilize soil. The clue to identifying this function are the internal structure (widest and best-built near the base) and the fact that it usually leans into the slope, with the most even face outward. The control of slope and soil was especially important along roads, which often were cut back into the slope to provide a flat roadbed. Hence, roads are associated with short sections of retaining walls built to anchor slopes, and simultaneously to protect them from erosion.

Cellar holes are a distinctive type of wall that served the dual purpose of being a foundation and a retaining wall. Normally they are small squares of stone, sunk into the ground on three or four sides, no longer on one side than forty feet. Another key feature of cellar holes is that they are often flanked by either a stepping stone or a doorsill on one end, and a collapsed fireplace on the other, which may be little more than a pile of stones, the clay that once held them being long reduced into ruins.

A small circular wall, commonly found above wells, eastern Massachusetts

A barway through a wall to a field, southern Vermont

A stepping stile for crossing a wall, eastern Connecticut

Foundation wall for an outbuilding, Concord, New Hampshire

Small stone enclosures—either circular or square—were often built to guard wells from erosion and pollution. Typically, they rise above grade from the stone-lined well below.

Walls built to impound water include dams, dikes, and levees. Because stone, especially dry-stone, is very porous, impoundment walls are always banked on one side by fine-grained earthen material to prevent leakage. They usually occur in low places along streams, rivers, and bottomlands. Their location, alone, is the most diagnostic criteria.

Walls are also built intentionally to divide property for any purpose. Usually they are simply stacked freestanding walls, either of single or double construction, equally high on either side, that extend away from the house-garden-barn-stockyard epicenter of the farmsteads. Typically they are lower than stockyard walls, less well laid than foundations, and much longer, having accumulated along fence lines, rather than the edges of buildings and pens. These are the most common walls in New England, typically built as stacks with multiple segments that surround and divide the most productive agricultural lands, usually tillage fields and mowing lands. Many division walls evolve into enclosure walls, but only after enclosure is complete. Adjacent land is usually free of stone.

Division walls adjacent to tillage fields usually have a greater abundance of smaller stones, either surmounting older sections or filling corners. Walls around pastures almost always were built more simply, single if there are fewer and more blocky stones, or double if there is an abundance of stone of mixed shape. Normally there are many residual stones left in the field. They also lack later piles of smaller stone.

Stone face of a small mill dam, showing soil liner and ledge, eastern Connecticut

Finally, walls are built as continuous monuments around property. Typically, these are better built and more massive than pasture walls, especially on established farmsteads. When they cross rough country, it indicates that stone disposal was less critical. Most often they are uncapped double walls.

Some walls, especially short ones that are similar on all sides, were built to enclose something. They function as fences. Those built to yard in livestock often extend away from barn foundations and come in a variety of shapes and sizes. Most often they are laid and battered, because they must be high enough and strong enough to contain and control large animals—horses, oxen, and hogs—in situations where the stock would other-

A bridge below a railroad spur to a quarry, southern New Hampshire

Town pound built of granite fieldstone, southern New Hampshire

wise move about (slaughter, breeding, fattening). Strength, height, and tightness are the key criteria. Almost all are either fully enclosed by stone or abut the remains of former barns. Enclosures built near the house usually framed gardens; they are usually well laid, because aesthetics, rather than containment, was most important. Those surrounding small family graveyards are low, complete in their enclosure, and often laid. Some grave markers may remain. In many cases, however, bodies were disinterred and moved into town, leaving only the odd wall as a clue. A pound is a special type of stone pen that served as a public jail for wandering livestock. Typically, they were built strong and high and were located along town roads.

Walls are also commonly associated with transportation corridors; as such, they are often more public, more massive, and better built than other wall types.

A wall for a roadside house that protected it from being crashed into, eastern Connecticut

Broadly, they fall into two groups: those that parallel roads, called roadside walls, and those that bridge something, called bridging walls. Many walls parallel farm and country roads, in part to get rid of the stone produced when the road was made, and that which was produced annually by traffic, runoff, and heave. Most roadside walls were built by crews working along both sides of the road at once, and hence appear similar on both sides. Something similar can be said for walls along canals and streams.

Other walls were built across patches of low ground crossed by streams. New England has thousands of small, generally collapsed stone culverts that grade upward in quality and size to stone bridges. When the crossing is nothing more than a pile of stone in a low swale, I refer to it as a stone ford. Stone causeways raise land, usually to create a dry roadbed above open water, marsh, and swamp.

A final purpose for building stone walls was some combination of guarding, exhibiting status, and aesthetics, here dubbed nonstructural architecture. Most common are low walls with tidy boundaries, clear-cut gates, and even faces that are expressions of pride. Taller walls often surround estates and were built principally for privacy. Both types are usually works of art.

CHAPTER 8

CHRONOLOGY AND AGE

Circumstantial evidence suggests overwhelmingly that the vast majority of historic New England stone walls were built by farmers, their hired hands, and their sons, daughters, and wives. We also know that many later walls built during the late nineteenth century and early twentieth century were built by immigrant tradesmen working in labor gangs. More recently, many of us have watched our neighbors, stonemasons, landscapers, work crews, and others building walls today in rural and suburban neighborhoods.

Beyond these generalities, however, very few stone walls, especially those on abandoned farms, have specific dates of origin. Hence, in order to learn the history of a favorite stone wall, we must reconstruct that history on our own, using on-the-ground detective work, which hopefully can be linked up to more remote documentary sources.

Most old New England stone walls have no specific calendar dates for their conception, construction, or completion. So, in lieu of good records, I recommend four separate techniques for building a history. The first way is to build a sequence of events (called a relative chronology) by arranging physical features of walls in the order in which they occurred, something often done by forensic detectives and archaeologists. Second is to find calendar ages that somehow relate to walls. For example, one might reasonably guess the wall was built after

Two stages of building (younger stacked wall on left and original laid wall on right), southern Vermont

the recording for the first deed to a property. A third method is to estimate and hopefully calibrate the processes that transform stone walls, such as the rate at which they are covered by lichens or strained by weathering. Fourth is to correlate the overall form and style of wall to a wall-building epoch, or cultural stage. This chapter presents these techniques, one by one.

SEQUENCING EVENTS

The most straightforward way to establish the age of a wall (or any aspect of it) is to place it within a sequence of events. Consider a well-built fieldstone wall with flat quarried capstones that is surmounted by a pile of stone potatoes. Although you don't know how old the wall is, you can deduce the sequence of events: the building of a fieldstone wall, the importing and placement of its capstones, then the later burial of the wall with waste stone. Another example might include recognizing the addition of a younger segment based on its abutting relationship to an older one. Anything that cuts a wall (for example, a road) must be younger. Anything that is contained within a wall (for example, a brick), must pre-date construction. Anything above a wall (for example, a rubble pile), must be younger.

Suppose you see two adjacent walls built of different materials; one solely with a conspicuously imported granite and the other of fieldstones with just a few granite slabs included. The fieldstone wall is probably the younger of the two, because it includes fragments of the other, whereas the reverse is not true.

Sequencing also applies to openings in walls. For example, many walls are built with intentional openings whose built ends are woven seamlessly into courses of stone in the wall; they were built simultaneously. An equal number of cases have openings that are younger than the wall; this can usually be seen as a break in construction techniques. Generally speaking, sequencing can be used to distinguish a wall that was built all at once (called a once-built wall) from one with more than one stage of construction (called a rebuilt wall). Walls are rebuilt for many reasons, as upgrading, repair, or the addition or subtraction of openings. A sequence of events determined in one place can often be correlated to a sequence in another, provided that they share one dated feature in common. Piecing such relationships together can yield fairly detailed local chronologies.

CALENDAR AGE

The second basic way of dating walls uses one or more calendar ages, either to fix a date for wall construction or to partition time into local epochs. A maximum limit age means that something is younger than the date in question. For example, the wall (archaeological walls excepted) in any town must be younger than the date the town was originally settled, let's say 1730. A minimum limiting age means that something is older than the date in question. For example, the agricultural walls on a property given up for back taxes and converted into a public park must be older than the date of conversion, let's say 1930. A bracketing age means you have both maximum and minimum limiting ages. For example, all of the original stone walls in the case above must have been built after the date of settlement but before the date of conversion, in other words, in the two centuries between 1730 and 1930.

Bracketing ages can be established for most properties in New England. For example, most towns have a generally accepted date of settlement, which often precedes incorporation. Many properties were once parts of large tracts for which legal documents exist. These are maximum ages. Within such towns, deeds to specific properties, especially in the nineteenth century, mention stone walls. The first mention of such walls yields a minimum age. Hence, the interval between first settlement and first mention yields a bracketing age. Often the goal in reconstructing wall history is to shorten the bracketing age from either end, perhaps by finding when a property was first subdivided into lots, or the date when land was deeded to a descendent.

For a specific calendar age for a wall segment, look for the mention of some aspect of wall construction in a primary source document. For public engineered structures such as mills and town pounds, an exact date is usually available, providing minimum or maximum ages for nearby undated walls. This is usually not the

Central section (lighter color) rebuilt after the installation of a culvert, eastern Connecticut

case for farmsteads because wall construction was part of an ongoing, often tedious process, not unlike gathering firewood, one that did not involve the exchange of money, which is usually the impetus for a written record. Searching for a calendar age is worth it, because it can attach an otherwise bracketed sequence to specific local events.

Calendar ages for individual farm walls range from very firm to very tenuous. In the best circumstances, a farmer's journal or account book may remark that a wall was built (more likely completed) on such-and-such a date, then give its dimensions or survey coordinates. At the other extreme, the same journal may only mention the hauling of stone somewhere on the farm. Good calendar dates for construction of farm walls can occasionally be obtained from receipts and invoices for services rendered, perhaps for the purchase of stone or the hiring of a mason. Tax records, which mention "improved" versus "unimproved" land, provide reasonable dates for the initialization of walls that may have actually taken some time to be completed.

Correlation of a specific feature in a stone wall to a specific dated event also helps build local history. For example, a wall that contains stone from a specific quarry has a maximum age fixed by the calendar date when the quarry first opened. However, the date at which the quarry closed may be irrelevant, because the stone could have been moved from one wall to another. Correlation ages can also be obtained from manufactured objects (usually bottles or metal tools) that were actually built into the wall during construction. One must watch out, however, for objects inserted into the void spaces well after the date of their manufacture. In these cases, however, the artifact usually provides a maximum age.

ABANDONMENT AGE

All walls corrode, fall apart, become covered by vegetation, and merge with the soil, given enough time. Calibrating the rate at which walls become tarnished and tumbled by natural processes gives us a completely independent type of dating called a wall's abandonment age. This technique assumes that a wall built over a certain period of time had an actual date of completion, and then was abandoned to the elements. Unfortunately, the rates of such changes can only be crudely calibrated, leaving us with four simple age categories: new, recent, old, and very old. *New* indi-

Example of brownstone block that has weathered at different rates, central Massachusetts

cates within the past few years; *recent,* the last few decades; *old,* a century or more; and *very old,* colonial in age.

There are two basic ways of estimating how long a wall has been undergoing change. First is to focus on the surface of the stones in an attempt to calibrate the degree of lichen cover and weathering. Second is to focus on the wall itself, the degree to which it has been damaged and buried.

Typically, a stone without lichens is a fresh stone. This is not true for smooth quartz boulders, which can survive centuries without a spot of lichen. However, any stone with a rough or granular surface that is exposed to some sun will be colonized, beginning with irregular splotches, then enlarging into all sorts of forms. Given enough time, lichens will cover nearly the entire stone surface. Many owners of new walls attempt to accelerate this aging process, washing their walls with garden fertilizer, diluted yogurt, or manure.

Unfortunately, the transition from completely uncovered to completely covered with lichen cannot yet be calibrated broadly in New England. Time is simply one of many variables that influence growth rate. Others include the composition of the stone (some lichens favor lime-rich rocks, whereas others hate them); the surface texture of the stone (rough surfaces are favored); exposure to sunlight (lichens grow fastest in full sun); the moisture regime (frequent rains help); the content of precipitation (from nutrient-rich dust to toxic metals or salt); the presence of herbivorous bacteria, fungi, insects, and small mammals; the degree of competition with other types of lichen; and finally, random acts of nature.

Though complex, lichen growth is one of the most conspicuous and earliest changes to help date a wall. For all practical purposes, a wall with a good coat of lichens is at least a few decades old; one with a continuous coat is likely a century or more.

Weathering of stone takes place slowly. All rock material exposed at the surface of the Earth is out of chemical equilibrium (it was created at high temperatures and pressures), and will therefore spontaneously change when exposed to air and water; living things are involved because they greatly accelerate the process. Bacteria produce crusts on the stones; lichens produce organic solvents that dissolve the most resistant minerals; and decomposing humus is leached like tea to produce a weak acid. All of this helps convert hard rock to clay and brown dust, given enough time. If the surface of the stone stays in-

Iron-rich fieldstones decomposing to rusty powder, eastern Connecticut

tact while it changes color, we use the term weathering rind. This is especially notable on smooth, dark, rounded stones, which remain intact as they sit in the wall, rather than the more mica-rich and coarse crystalline stones, which usually crumble and split.

The best weathering rinds occur on basalt, painting a vivid orange color on the outside of otherwise dark, somewhat green-tinged stones. The color is essentially that of rust, which results from the combination of raw (reduced) iron in dark minerals, oxygen in the air, and water. Granite also produces a weathering rind, but it is often chalky white, bleaching crystals that often otherwise have a pinkish hue. All rinds thicken with time at a decelerating rate.

One problem in assigning a weathering age to a wall is that the technique works only on freshly exposed or broken stone. Any bleached rind on granite or an orange-brown rind on basalt that is more than a millimeter thick means that the wall is fairly old. One of the best arguments against the alleged great antiquity of some walls claimed to be millennia old is that the most highly weathered stones they contain are not anywhere nearly as weathered as those surfaces that have stood exposed above the soil since deglaciation.

Another common manifestation of weathering is granular disintegration, in which the crystals, usually sand-sized, progressively fall away from the stone. This process is related to weathering rinds because it is usually the outer part of the rind that disintegrates as its inward part keeps developing. Disintegration depends on composition. In granite rocks, small dark grains (mafics, garnets, and magnetite) go first, followed by feldspars. In schists, metal sulfides, calcium-bearing minerals, and micas go first. The loss of these provides water with access to the interior of the stone, which increases the breakdown from frost and chemical solution. Sometimes rocks become porous, supported only by the intersecting framework of resistant materials, usually quartz. Such a rock might be crushed when stepped upon. Sandstones and conglomerates fall apart as the cement dissolves.

Often a hard spot in otherwise weak stones weathers into a standout, perhaps a quartz vein or a zenolith. Large standouts usually mean a deeply weathered stone. Of course, stones split with time as well, especially those that are well layered. Falling-apart stones suggest antiquity.

Mortar also provides a clue to the age of a wall. When fresh, cement has a conspicuous chalky, smooth, hard exterior. With time, however, the sand grains become exposed, the surface darkens, and it begins to more closely resemble rock. As mortared walls weather, gaps develop between the stones and the cement. Wide gaps indicate a fairly old though still-mortared wall. The cement itself indicates a dating since the time of the Civil War, when it came into widespread use.

Beyond lichen growth, staining, and chemical disintegration of the stones, all walls fall apart, even those that were well built and made from the most durable stones. The most obvious change in the form of a wall is when stones from the top layer simply fall out of position, rolling and sliding to the side or simply hanging on for their dear lives. Clearly, the degree to which this has occurred is as dependent on the quality of construction as on elapsed time; some very old walls still stand high. More important than its age, the presence of offset, slipped, and fallen stones indicates that the wall is not being maintained.

There are other processes that damage walls. Most insidious is the gradual spread of a double wall at its base. Most noticeable are the gaps knocked out by falling trees. Most unpredictable is frost heaving, which shows up here and there.

The most obvious clue to a recent wall is its connection to a new house, road, or building. This is not a fail-safe clue, however, because most modern building developments take place on old farmsteads or on historic properties, especially parks. On recent walls lichens are absent, or just beginning to dot the stone. Mortar, if present, is chalky gray and lacks exposed sand grains. If a wall is rebuilt from field-stones, some lichens on the original stone will still be present, often as dead crusts. Remnant of soil will still be present in the previously buried parts of the stone, often in cracks and indentations. Quarry dust is often present as well. Fresh surfaces, produced by scrapes from heavy equipment, random breaks, or hammer blows from the mason, will still look fresh, except for traprock, which will have a slight patina.

For a decades-old wall, the best clues come from the stones themselves. Their surface colors are still quite contrasting, with natural browns and grays being very different. Lichens are common on most stones, though not falling off or crusting entire surfaces. Trees have sprouted near the base of the wall. Some of the stacked stones have shifted out of position. All surfaces have at least a slight patina. Decomposed woody debris is quite common. Piles of nut leavings from rodents are common. None of the original soil or quarry dust is present.

For a centuries-old wall, everything listed above is included, but more intensely. Wall segments have likely fallen or sagged. Tree damage is clear, often from rooted trees against the wall. The lichen cover is usually extensive, with a variety of forms, crustose and foliose in equal abundance. The grade for uphill slopes is higher than for lower ones. The stones are covered with a weathering surface; naked stones are only those composed of quartz. Slaty stones have crumbled in place, sometimes as stacks of slabs held together only by gravity.

The self-published literature on stone walls is replete with millennium-old walls, which may very well exist. Unfortunately, none have yet been verified by physical evidence supported by peer-reviewed scientific studies with either radiocarbon dates or unambiguous archaeological associations.

CULTURAL STAGE

During the settlement of New England, the conversion of the land from the original condition of old-growth forest to the modern condition passed through predictable cultural stages, regardless of when it was initiated or how many stages were experienced. The process began with pioneering farmsteads and ends with the modern walls being built today. Each of these stages is associated with a certain pattern of stone walls on the landscape. Finding these patterns and relating them to local history provides a fourth method of assessing the chronology of stone walls.

Consider, for example, a primitive pile of stone along a fence line. This feature can be found on almost any farm, even on parts of well-developed estates. When this style of wall is the culminating condition for a property's stonework, however, we can be fairly sure that the place never developed past the pioneering stage. Some places, like Boston, passed through the pioneering stage by the late seventeenth century and were never abandoned. Others, like the interior valleys of Vermont, weren't settled until the early nineteenth century and were then abandoned after only a generation. In other cases—for example, Acadia, Maine—settlement began very early, but remained fairly primitive until it quickly passed into estate-style building, when the area was a playground for the wealthy. In other words, the bracketing dates for a cultural stage varies locally, being generally later and shorter the further one moves north or inland from the coast or large rivers.

In many documented cases the actual person who built a wall, or who contracted for its construction, is unambiguously known. For every one of these cases, however, there are thousands of other cases where the individual identity of a wall's builders cannot be known. We can, however, assign a cultural stage, based on the appearance of the wall.

The pre-European stage (before A.D. 1620) was characterized by the absence of stone walls. There were, however, specific stone structures, including monuments, weirs, local storage facilities, barricades, and burial mounds. They were built by pre-European inhabitants, almost certainly the Native American, largely Algonquin stock that has lived on this continent from some time after deglaciation; some are radiocarbon-dated to thousands of years old, and do not resemble the stonework of the earliest Norse settlement on the northern tip of Newfoundland. There is no evidence for European visitors to New England before the onset of late-fifteenth-century exploration.

The pioneering stage generally took place during the late seventeenth century in coastal villages, the early eighteenth century over most of the plateau, and the early nineteenth in the hinterlands. Dominated by stone as refuse, the walls seldom move beyond the dumped degree of order. Stone piles and residual stones are common, with mounds of small stones on larger ones. No farms stayed in this stage, though many were abandoned before the next stage was reached. Nearly all of these pioneering walls were built by the owners and residents of individual farms. Fathers, wives, sons, daughters, their neighbors, and their kin built millions of wall segments, generally from the generation that came after forest clearing but before abandonment. They are essentially family walls.

Stone piles from the early pioneering stage, inland Maine

The established farm stage is generally dated from the American Revolution (ca. 1776–83) to 1825–35. This was a period when early American farms were most successful and widespread. During slack times, farmers took the stone refuse of the earlier stage, using it to build a variety of walls, including elegant boundary walls and well-developed stone foundations, and quite a number of high stone fences. The stacked and laid degree of order is most common. Though many of these walls were built by families, probably just as many were hired out to work gangs, generally the unemployed or marginally employed, meaning those in need of work. Prisoners, slaves, laborers, Indian communities, and land-bound sailors also hired themselves out to improve what had earlier been a carnage of stone on certain properties. Walls built by gangs can be differentiated from family walls by their longer segments and more uniform construction, by the inclusion of more artifacts in the walls, and by a greater degree of sophistication.

The forest-and-city stage coincides roughly

A well cover from the established farm stage, eastern Connecticut

Ornamental turrets, which usually date from the forest-and-city stage, coastal Maine

with a century of decline in farm wealth and rural inland population, and the concomitant rise in wealth of the industrialized urban population. This stage began about 1825, with the beginning of transportation improvements—canals, railroads, and turnpikes—that helped pull farmers' sons and daughters off family farms toward the cities. It ended for good during the 1930s, during America's Great Depression, when most of the remaining farmsteads, struggling to hold on as dairy farms, were finally abandoned.

There were two conspicuous trends in stone-wall construction during this era. First, near centers of industry, walls did not decay but continued to be built up on estates, especially by immigrant tradesmen, especially between the massive European immigration of the late nineteenth century and the stock-market crash of 1929, including the Victorian era, the Gilded Age, and the Jazz Age. With a vastly uneven supply of money and a surplus of cheap labor, the wealthy purchased property near industrial cities and moved out to "cottages" and rural properties to summer

Elaborate stonework from the forest-and-city stage, Newport, Rhode Island

away from the grime of commerce. Specific wall-building traditions of the Irish, Italian, and Indian are reported, but largely unstudied. This trend coincided with a second trend that took place away from such centers of influence, however, where rural properties were abandoned, and where the walls became ruins.

The final reclamation stage took place gradually, beginning with the availability of personal automobiles in the earliest years of the twentieth century. First came the reinvigoration of country life during the first few decades of the twentieth century, during which rural properties were reclaimed; stonework repair was part of that colonial revival. Then came the onset of the environmental movement, which brought thousands of young people into old properties to repair walls. Finally, during the construction boom and rapid sprawl of the last few decades of the twentieth century, many walls were built, often using materials from old stone walls. Many of these are not tradesmen walls but were built by the property owners, generally well-educated people who built walls in their spare time for outdoor fun.

When I first began to look at walls twenty years ago, I had several colleagues who claimed to be able to distinguish colonial walls from what are called American walls, those of the early nineteenth century. I cannot. Instead, what I see are two basic populations of walls, an earlier version of dumped and stacked walls of primitive construction and limited continuity, and a later version of more well-built walls, with more even faces, most of which were stacked, but much more evenly. The conversion of walls from the earlier version to the later version often coincided with the change from colonial to American walls, but that wasn't always the case. Walls might simply be upgraded when the opportunity presented itself, regardless of the calendar year this actually occurred. The correlation between wall form and historical version holds true, but there is so much overlap that the distinction isn't that useful.

The myth of the tumbledown wall is related to the alleged distinction between colonial and American walls, which are said to be primitive and well-built, respectively. Many tumbledown walls do in fact represent the faded glory of formerly higher walls. But most were never built up in the first place. Instead, they represent the dumped stage or simple stacks. Also, tumbling is only one of many mechanisms that bring a wall down. Many sag instead. A heavily capped double wall, especially if built on frost-susceptible or soft soil, splits as the halves move apart.

Corner piles, indicating operation after farm mechanization, southern New Hampshire

With the capstone pushing the wall downward and the expanding soils pushing the sides apart, the wall splays into a broad, flaring shape. Our bias is to believe that our antecedents did a good job originally, and that nature has since taken the walls apart. The truth is that many walls were built as linear landfills, then stayed that way. We know this because well-built walls in the Old World have stood proudly for millennia.

CHAPTER 9

CLASSIFICATION AND NAMING

Early European travelers made informal distinctions between the ugly walls they encountered in the fields and along roadsides, and the orderly walls of village centers. A later colonial distinction was made between what was called a "tossed" wall and a built wall. Another common informal distinction was made between a single wall (whose stones are merely set atop one another) and a double wall (built with stones from opposite sides slanting inward toward each other). Finally, farmers often made a distinction between a pasture wall (usually single and tottering) and a field wall (which was more massive and well built). Though these distinctions are clear, they were all based on different criteria. None of these distinctions are mutually exclusive; for example, a pasture wall need not be ugly, nor does a field wall need to be built from both sides.

This chapter presents a classification system or taxonomy for naming stone walls and related phenomenon. It is designed to yield a consistent set of names that can be easily applied, based on observation rather than interpretation. All classification systems are compromises between rigidity in naming protocols (which

Boulder dots (stone line), northern New Hampshire

A simple stack of stones, Berkshires, Massachusetts

Stone veneer used to prevent erosion, Winnepesauke district, New Hampshire

makes the rules easy to follow) and flexibility (which allows for the wiggle room of real life).

To qualify as a stone wall, an object must meet four criteria: material (natural or artificial stone); continuity (no conspicuous gaps); elongation (four times longer than wide); and height (either knee-high or stacked).

In biology, all living things are grouped into categories of different rank, ranging from the largest to the smallest, from kingdom, phylum, class, order, family, and genus on down to species. I propose something similar for stone-wall science. For the largest group, I use the term *stone domain*, which includes all notable stones and collections of notable stones, whether modern or ancient, tall or short, piles and walls, towers and turrets. ("Notable" doesn't specify a size, composition, or concentration. Rather, the stone or group of stones is differentiated from those in the soil. A ledge is excluded because it is bedrock.)

The domain of stone consists of four major classes: walls, rows (low or gapped alignment), concentrations (including piles and monuments), and notable stones (typified by the isolated boulders or quarried slabs so frequently adorning new construction). However, I have focused entirely on stone walls in this taxonomy. There are six families of stone walls: freestanding, flanking, raising, impoundment, foundation, and confinement. Each of these is further subdivided into types and subtypes.*

No taxonomy is ever complete; otherwise it would include as many categories as objects. There is always a need to describe individual objects at a finer level than the subdivision allows. Consider the case of the classic double wall, which is a subtype (classic) within a type (double), within the family (freestanding), within a class (wall). It could be mortared or unmortared, built of fieldstone or quarrystone, or be capped or uncapped. To encompass all of these common features in a single taxonomy would require a minimum of eight different variants of a classic double wall, rather than one.

Instead of adding more categories, I suggest the following order in describing the finer details of stone walls:

- Condition (damaged or undamaged, etc.)
- Degree of order (stacked, dumped, or laid, etc.)
- Stone topography (boulder, slab, chunky)
- Stone source (fieldstone vs. quarrystone)
- Structure (single vs. double, etc.)
- Function (foundation, retaining, etc.)

Stone pavement (flat veneer), used for a patio, southern New Hampshire

For example, the wall I see most often, just east of my house, is a partially collapsed, crudely stacked, slabby fieldstone double wall.

*The appendix Classification Key presents criteria for distinguishing the families and types for all four classes of stone objects. Additional information about classification of rows, concentrations, and notable stones is available from the Web site of the Stone Wall Initiative at *http://web.uconn.edu/stonewall,* accessible through the alias *http://stonewall.uconn.edu.*

STONE WALLS

FREESTANDING WALLS

Stone bands. The most primitive type of free-standing wall is little more than a low mound—really an elongate pile—of stone that is usually neither straight nor of uniform width and which, in most cases, accumulated piecemeal beneath a fence line. It scarcely qualifies as a wall. Typically, its stones are dumped, rather than stacked, though there is a constant variation. Sometimes the trace of the stone band is highly irregular. Wavy stone bands result when a straight line wasn't used to guide the dumping of stone. Beaded stone bands (alternately thick and thin) form when individual piles or dumps of stone occur along a straight line. Sometimes this happened when the stones were selectively thrown below fence posts, rather than under rails.

Single walls. The most common type of stone wall is the single wall, sometimes called the pasture wall or farmer's wall. Although this is often two or more stones wide at the base, the dominant theme is that of a single stack. (There is only one common, unnamed subtype of the single wall; a seemingly random collection of stones stacked one above the other.) When possible, the stones are placed so that the outer face is more uniform than toward the middle, as if they were

Southwestern Highlands: mix of hard and soft rock, western Massachusetts

A millstone, often used as decoration, eastern Connecticut

wedges, being laid with the short side of the triangle on the outside, its point in the middle.

Sometimes the shape of the stones exerts sufficient control on the single wall to produce distinctive special subtypes. First is the cordwood
wall, which is built of prisms of stone laid end-
wise across the wall, so they resemble split firewood. These occur only where the bedrock
geology produced odd-shaped stones, usually
tightly folded slate or hexagonal columns of
basalt. Most evocative is the lace wall, which is
especially common on Martha's Vineyard. Often
wider at the base, lace walls are built of equant
but odd-shaped stones in such a way that the top
of the wall resembles lace. The cannonball wall, a
close cousin of the lace wall, is made of unusually
rounded, even-sized stones. (See photo p. 62.)

Double walls. The most familiar, respected
type of wall is the double wall. Its diagnostic element is the presence of at least two lines of stone
laid or stacked close against one another such
that the stones slant inward toward the center,
which is often filled with rubble. A double wall
may be capped or uncapped. There are two basic

*Intact chimney of a former house,
southern Connecticut*

subtypes of double wall. The classic double wall is stacked, rather than carefully laid,
and usually thigh-high or lower. Built from both sides, it lacks the architectural or
artistic refinement that would qualify it as an ornate wall. Most classic double walls
are exterior boundary walls for prosperous but middle-class farms. If capped at all,
they are capped with fieldstone, culled for its tabular shape and large size.

An ornate double wall is a common but highly variable subtype of double wall,
distinguished by being ornamented in some conspicuous way, usually to display
wealth or status. An ornate wall need not be ostentatious, though many are. Most
were laid rather than stacked, and architectural and aesthetic concerns rather than
stone disposal or territorialism were paramount. Expensive to build, ornate double

walls are often called estate walls, especially when they are high and associated with hedges. The most common variant of the ornate double wall is the quarry-stone-capped wall. Perhaps the most common style around public cemeteries, this is identified by quarried stone blocks, usually granite, marble, or sandstone, laid on a fieldstone base. Slightly less common is the quarrystone wall, which is built entirely of quarried stone and is therefore by definition an ornate wall. Copestone walls are also common, especially in colonial-era English towns. These were built by placing the final tier of stones on edge across the double wall to produce a fencelike top (related to spikes, hedges, and broken glass) that prevents climbing or sitting on the wall. Most ornate of all is the turreted wall, in which pedestals resembling the turrets on medieval castles are built into the wall, clearly for show. The guard wall is ornate by virtue of its height of more than five feet, and it usually includes other ornamentation.

Broad walls. The wall exceeds the width required for structural support in a double wall, which is typically about two and a half feet wide at the base. Normally a third line of stone is present. The subtype disposal wall is essentially a double wall with an extra-wide middle zone, commonly about ten feet wide, but which may be as much as thirty feet. The center is usually filled with dumped and tossed stones and rubble, with no effort given to its arrangement. These are clearly the result of a planned single clearing effort, usually a capital improvement on a farm. Only rarely are disposal walls ornate. A subtype of broad wall is the once-again wall, which contains an additional line of stone laid against a previous wall. Most common is a classic double wall flanked by a heap of stones stacked or tossed on one side. This is diagnostic of the reactivation of fields, especially orchards, where a renewed effort at capital improvement took place, usually with tractor loaders. A very distinctive though rare subtype of a broad wall is the walking wall, which is essentially a raised sidewalk. Its diagnostic elements are the presence of both enormous tabular capstones and pedestrian access via a stile or stairway. Considering the severity of the mud season in much of New England and the frequent trips made between house, barn, and stockyard, walking walls were often worth the effort. (See bottom photo p. 61.)

Abutting walls. The final type of freestanding wall is the abutting wall, created by a continuous line of single stones at least two feet high. The most common subtype is the boulder wall made of boulders simply rolled, then levered into place, touching each other. Slightly less common is the rock slab wall, built with jagged blocks rather than boulders, and almost always placed with twentieth-century construction equipment. Rare, but even more distinctive, is the stone pale wall, built of slabs inserted into the ground like standing stones, but abutting each other. (See photo p. 198.)

FLANKING WALLS

This family contains the second most common type of stone walls. They flank a slope, usually at a break in the slope, rather than standing freely above grade. These walls are built to stabilize a bank, either by holding back the earth or by protecting it from erosion, and commonly by both.

Retaining walls. A retaining wall is often found in village, garden, and barnyard settings. It is defined by its asymmetry—high on one side and low (usually at grade) on the other. The most common subtype is the below-grade retaining wall, which supports an excavated face cut below grade. Less common is the above-grade retaining wall, which supports a face backfilled behind the wall to produce a flat space at higher elevation. Modern retaining walls in gardens and landscaped yards are often curved. Older ones were usually straight. The structure of most retaining walls, designed principally to hold back the earth, is that of an inverted wedge of stone, thickest at the base, where most of the support is needed. Usually they are laid rather than tossed because of the extra strength required. Extra care is commonly given to drainage at their bases, most often accomplished with a heap of rubble tossed on the uphill side. Most are designed with a battered face leaning uphill, especially when the wall partitions a continuous slope and the stones are poorly shaped for building. False re-

Flanking (armoring) wall, which prevents erosion, inland Maine

taining walls were originally built freestanding, but have since collected enough earth on their upslope ends to be indistinguishable from a poorly built retaining wall. (See bottom photo p. 64.)

Well guards are a special subtype of the retaining wall. At its most primitive, a well guard is little more than a low circular or square rim of stones built just above ground level to prevent the washing in of debris or the entry of animals into the otherwise potable water supply. In many cases, however, the stone foundation extends deep below the ground as a lining for the well; such a foundation might otherwise be called a facing wall (a type of armoring wall) because it serves to prevent erosion or a retaining wall because it keeps soil from slumping and flowing into the well, especially when the water table rises during snowmelt and runoff. Sometimes the stone is arranged in the form of a vertical arch, so the pressure of the earth directed inward toward the well is supported by the arrangement of stones.

Armoring wall. A common type of flanking wall, the armoring wall protects the land from erosion, rather than solely holding back earth. A subtype is the riprap wall, a wedge of stone usually dumped against the base of a sea cliff, an eroding shore, or a stream bank, wherever floods and coastal storms threaten the land. Another subtype is the facing wall, built to provide a regular, resistant face against the force of erosion. There are two common variants of facing walls: the seawall, usually built above a riprap wall, and the stream-bank wall. Both are designed to prevent erosion from the side. Mill dams, though built with an even face, are not included in this group. The stones of their tail races often are, however.

RAISING WALLS

These walls are designed to create and maintain a ridge or plateau of soil above normal grade, usually on land that is flat rather than sloping. They share similarities with above-grade retaining walls.

Raised beds. Most common are raised bed walls, which need not be more than a stack of stones of any enclosed shape that hold up the raised beds of gardens.

Raised land. These walls were built to raise land above swampy or marshy soils, or above the water itself. In most cases the stone was hauled in and dumped to create a narrow, solid, artificial strip of land on which a range of activities took place. Subtypes include the causeway, built to create a transportation corridor across wet ground, usually a marsh; the stone groin, built perpendicular to a shoreline to prevent coastal erosion and maintain a beach by trapping sand; the stone jetty, a pair of stone walls flanking a navigable tidal channel and designed to prevent sedimentation; the stone breakwater used to protect a harbor; and the stone pier, designed as a platform where ships may exchange cargo. These types are defined more by function than by structure. A final subtype is the edging wall, which protects a raised area (like a filled tidal marsh) rather than a corridor. It is related to an above-ground retaining wall.

Raised land (breakwater) wall used for harbor protection, Block Island, Rhode Island

Bridging walls. Another common type of raising wall that was built over small streams. A subtype is the culvert wall, which was usually built on the upstream and downstream sides of a central fill of rubble or stone, through which a stone culvert was placed. Primitive culverts were usually created by placing elongate stones parallel to the stream, then capping them with a tier of more tabular cross stones. The difference between a culvert wall and a stone bridge wall is that the latter is built to span a stream, rather than to convey it through a stone pipe surrounded by fill. (See bottom photo p. 85.)

IMPOUNDMENT WALLS

The family of impoundment walls is designed to hold back water, rather than soil, usually to create a permanent pond for downstream millworks or, more recently, as a flood-control measure. Because stone is porous when stacked, impoundment walls require some sort of impermeable lining, which is usually provided by fine earth, often muck or silt dredged locally from a marsh or clay bank. Hence, impoundment walls serve primarily as a retaining wall for artificial fill. Structurally, they are similar to above-grade retaining walls and causeway walls, though the stone is present to control water erosion as much as to hold back the impermeable materials creating the impoundment.

Stone dikes. These walls were built to protect low ground against a rising flood. Usually built as simple retaining walls, backfilled with earth on the side facing rising water, stone dikes are most often seen around natural meadows, which were cut for hay that would otherwise be ruined by a late-summer flood.

Mill dams. In New England, the stone ruins of old dams are almost as evocative as the tumbled freestanding farm wall. Built across streams and rivers of various sizes, old mill dams—many of which have since been restored—convey the ambience of colonial and early American village settings. A variety of stonework is usually associated with the foundation for the mill building and with the chutes through which the water was directed to flow toward and away from the wheel or turbine. (See top photo p. 85.)

Pooling walls: A final type of impoundment wall was created in high places to store water for later use, fed by gravity. This type includes cisterns, designed mainly to catch rainwater. Unlike mill dams, pooling walls are usually raised above the ground on all sides. They are analogous to raised beds, but raise water instead of soil.

FOUNDATION WALLS

Foundation walls were built to support something from below, usually a building, usually on two or more sides. Their diagnostic feature is that the top course of stones was laid as close to horizontal as possible, in order to support the basal beams and sills. This usually required some care, so foundation walls are typically laid rather than tossed. Foundation walls are often cut into the slope on the uphill side, and thus frequently share traits with retaining walls, to which they are closely related.

Cellar holes. The most evocative foundation wall is the cellar hole. Each is the grave of an abandoned house. House foundations, even on flat land, were usually excavated at least several feet into the ground in order to create a cellar that could be used to store food under cool but unfrozen conditions. After a hole was excavated, the cellar was faced off with stone, laid in courses to a height where the basal timbers would rest. One end of the cellar foundation was usually built up into a fireplace, usually also made of stone, most of which have since collapsed. The weight of the overlying building is what holds most cellar foundations in place against the pressure of the creeping soil. Hence, with the buildings gone, most cellar holes eventually collapse inward.

Building foundations. Most wooden buildings had stone foundations. Far and away the most common are the subtype of barn foundations, which are recognized by their larger footprints than those for houses. On slopes, most building foundations were excavated back into the earth, producing a walk-in half cellar, which was sometimes large enough to serve as a separate level holding livestock. This group also includes the foundations of large houses, some of which did not have cellars, and some of which kept going upward to be the walls of stone houses. These are dubbed house foundations, to distinguish them from cellar holes though the subtypes grade into each other. Another subtype, outbuilding foundations, were seldom excavated into the ground; instead courses of stone were raised on the downhill sides and corners of buildings of various sizes—garages, sheds, cribs, haystacks, and even outhouses.

CONFINEMENT WALLS

In the family of confinement walls, the emphasis is not on the wall but on the space created by short wall segments on three or more sides. The boundary between a small field with freestanding walls and a large pen with confinement walls is, unfortunately, arbitrary.

Stone pens. These are generally small, unroofed enclosures bounded by stone on at least three sides, ranging from about twenty feet to about one hundred feet long on each side. All were used to contain animals for some purpose. The most interesting subtype is the stone pound, essentially a heavy-duty public jail for wayward livestock, almost always located on or near a public road. The walls are built of massive stones and/or laid with extra care to ensure durability and structural stability. Another subtype is the stone corral, which is more general in function, and can be located anywhere on a farm. Large variations of this type are sometimes referred to as stone yards. Sometimes laid and sometimes tossed, stone corrals served to partition space for feeding, breeding, slaughtering, nursing, and culling, usually in the vicinity of the barn. The stone fold is the outbuilding equivalent of the corral, into which sheep were folded for protection. (See top photo p. 86.)

Ring walls. These small, unroofed, circular enclosures do not qualify as pounds or pens, usually because they are much too low. They are among the most difficult type of confinement wall to classify because they barely qualify as walls and because of a continuum in size and form, from disintegrating stacks that once surrounded a campfire to very well built, vertically walled enclosures more than fifty feet in diameter. Small, poorly built rings grade into piles. The subtype fire ring is easy to recognize because the stones are arranged into a circular stack and are distinctly cracked, split, charred, and reddened by the fire's heat. Larger ones were built to help contain charcoal or potash fires, which needed to burn slowly for days, and therefore required extra care in confinement. Charcoal was a vital fuel for home heating and colonial manufacturing before the widespread availability of coal, and long before anyone thought forest denudation was a bad thing. A second subtype of ring wall is the stone circle, which does not contain fire-cracked stones, and which is highly variable. Closest to typical freestanding walls are those originally built to surround a large shade tree that has since disappeared. Stone circles range from architectural structures and guides for horse mills to benches and decorative borders.

Stone chambers. This rare type of wall includes any and all enclosures that were roofed, often with stone. This is also the most enigmatic group of all, including as it does dozens of stone chambers alleged to be everything from simple root cellars to meditation huts. In this category are also stone passageways and underground stone-roofed tunnels, which are rare as well. (See photo p. 149.)

PART III

WALLS IN SPACE AND TIME

Fieldstone granite near Mount Monadnock in New Hampshire

CHAPTER 10

STONE-WALL LANDSCAPES

The distribution of stone walls on the landscape is not entirely lawless. Instead, there are consistent patterns between the type, size, and concentration of stone walls and the lay of the land. This occurs at three different scales: that of terrain (hilltop to valley bottom), that of stone-wall provinces (towns and counties), and that of sub-regions (equivalent in size to states).

TERRAIN

Over much of New England, the highest elevations often contain resistant ledges of rock. When these occur at a summit, they are called balds. Though rock seems to be everywhere, stone walls in such places are strangely absent. Normally, this is because the terrain was too rocky and steep to farm, so there was no need to build walls. In these highest, rockiest areas, surface stones were most likely swept away by glacial and gravitational erosional processes rather than by depositional ones. Walls present in such places are usually property boundary markers, built not so much as an adjunct to farming as to boldly mark the edge of a large landholding. Classic double walls, spaced too far apart to see one from another, are the standard walls in such terrain. Mount Monadnock, New Hampshire, may be the best place to see such walls.

At the next topographical level down are New England's proverbial rolling hills, which were often streamlined by the ice in a northwest-to-southeast direction. This terrain is almost always underlain by hardpan (lodgment till), a compact, concretelike substance that is dominantly sandy clay and silt, but which also contains a good supply of stones. Walls on lodgment till are common, if not nearly

Upland terrain, which yields well-built, widely spaced walls, eastern Connecticut

ubiquitous, as stones were released slowly by erosion and frost heaving throughout the entire life of a farm. Glacial erratics, larger and rounder than most of the till stones, are common as well. Stone walls were usually built in this setting because hardpan soils were prized for pasture and tillage. They are not, however, nearly as massive as those farther down; nor are they set as close together.

Only after leaving the rolling uplands do we enter the valley environment. During deglaciation, the tops of the hills were exposed first; each was an island of ice-free terrain that enlarged as the glacier melted downward, rapidly at first, then more slowly. Water erosion was concentrated at the midpoint, where the slope was the steepest. Hence, it is here, on the valley sides, that glacially transported stone, including erratics, is most concentrated on the landscape. Walls built on these hillsides are more "lawless" (Thoreau's word), chaotic, massive, and highly concentrated than those either above or below them. It is in these places that some of the poorest pastures are located, without benefit of the gentler slopes of the lodgment till nor of the meltwater deposits below them.

Valley-side terrain, which often yields massive pasture walls, eastern Connecticut

The meltwater zone lies below the valley sides of land within the ice. Here glacial gravel, washing down from the enlarging islands, nearly filled the bottoms of many small valleys. Residual pieces of stagnant ice often remained when the sediment infill took place; mantled with muddy gravel, these blocked stream drainage to lower parts of the valley. Around most such stagnant blocks of ice were moatlike lakes that deepened as the ice melted downward, and which were incrementally filled by sand and gravel pouring in from above and from the north.

Eventually, even the most deeply buried blocks of stagnant ice melted away, allowing valleys to drain southward to lakes or to the sea. Along the shorelines of the former moat-shaped lakes were thousands of well-drained, boulder-studded terraces left high and dry above the bottomland marshes and meadows. These flat-topped, gravel-filled benches, which occurred at many levels, are locally known as kame terraces. Because they were flat, well drained, set parallel to the edges of valleys, and often covered with windblown dust, they provided excellent sites for spring pasture and tillage fields (though they would dry out in the late summer). Stone walls in these places are usually little more than sprawling, triangular piles of boulders and cobbles.

Final melting of the stagnant ice often exposed a ridge of very coarse gravel set parallel to the streams. These ridges are eskers, places where the meltwater flowed with full glacial force within tunnels beneath the ice sheet. Because esker water was icy cold and full of grit, and because it was flowing under pressure, eskers were capable of transporting large concentrations of rounded boulders. Eskers often stand out as sinuous, bony ridges above otherwise stone-free sand and marsh; their walls look as if they were built of watermelons.

Below the meltwater zone, an abrupt scarp usually leads down to the floodplains proper, which are muddy, marshy, swampy, and often stone-free. These plains, especially in larger valleys, were the first to be grazed by livestock, because they formed natural meadows,

Glacial meltwater boulders, Stafford, Connecticut

Valley-bottom walls are in millworks rather than fields, eastern Connecticut

places where persistent high water and/or seasonal flooding prevented tree growth. These bottomlands, especially next to small streams, usually have alternating narrow and broad reaches, making the valley appear beaded when seen from above. Narrow reaches of fast-flowing water with huge in-channel boulders and exposed bedrock alternate with broader stone-free reaches where flood-waters were able to spread out and cover the lowland.

Narrow reaches were often the sites of small mill dams and the accompanying stonework of mill villages: chutes, building foundations, abutments, and tail races. Such stonework is often composed of a mixture of quarried stone and local fieldstone. Broad reaches, called interval lands, usually lack stone walls because there was no stone, especially when they are very wet. In many cases, however, walls descending from the valley sides continued across the meadows to divide property; many have since become partially, if not completely, buried by flood deposits. In larger streams that drain into salt water, the zone of seasonal flooding is replaced by the zone of permanent submergence caused by the rise of sea level since deglaciation. Muddy tide flats and salt marshes typically lack stone walls, unless they are truly ancient and therefore built before the sea rose to submerge them.

STONE-WALL PROVINCES

A stone-wall province is a town-sized-or-larger area where the constellation of stone walls is or should be similar, based on the area's bedrock, glacial background, and human history. (See maps in the appendix Stone-Wall Provinces.) The three sources I used to define provinces were: a geological highway map for the northeastern United States, a surface materials map published by the U.S. Geological Survey, and maps of settlement history published in the National Atlas. (Complete citations are in the appendix Additional Resources.)

I generalized the bedrock-type map into three basic terrains underlain by rocks that produce: blocky stones (granite and gneiss), slabby stones (schist and quartzite), and few stones (soft rock). I generalized the glacial surface materials map into places where the terrain is very rocky (shallow bedrock), smeared with glacial till (lodgment till), covered by bumpy moraines (moraine), buried by sand and gravel (sand and gravel), buried by fine-grained mud (fines), or partly buried by a mixture of fines or something else (mixed). I generalized the settlement history map into four basic units equivalent to the wall-building cultural stages: places generally with no historic stone walls (unsettled before 1890), places with rough walls of the pioneering stage (settled 1800–1890), places with well-built walls of the established farm stage (settled 1700–1800), and places with a mixture of farmstead, estate, and urban walls of the forest-and-city stage (settled before 1700).

Using the maps titled Bedrock Type and Glacial Surface Materials provided in the appendix Stone-Wall Provinces, I have identified eleven types of stone-wall provinces. The simplest one to understand is the Island province. Except for imported stone, all walls built on the soft rock of the coastal plain—Provincetown to Staten Island—lie on the well-defined moraines, which contain stone dragged in from areas to the north. Next in simplicity is the Imported province, which coincides with areas mapped as Fines. This is because there is no natural surface stone in this unit. The remaining nine provinces are all possible combinations of three types of bedrock and three types of glacial action. For naming purposes, I substitute the familiar terms "granite" for terrain of the map unit Granite and Gneiss, and the term "fieldstone" for the more mixed-rock assemblage in the unit Schist and Quartzite. To keep things simple, I did not further subdivide the provinces by cultural stage. Rather, one can just expect walls to be more massive, better built, and elaborate as cultural stages rise from pioneering, to established farm, to forest and city, then to reclamation.

The Granite Block province occurs where the bedrock unit Granite and Gneiss coincide with shallow bedrock: Granite Mix and Granite Boulder provinces occur where this same rock unit coincides with Lodgment Till and Sand and Gravel, respectively. The Fieldstone Slab province occurs where the bedrock unit Schist and Quartzite coincide with shallow bedrock. Fieldstone Mix and Fieldstone Boulder provinces occur where this same rock unit coincides with Lodgment Till and Sand and Gravel, respectively. The Softrock Highland province occurs where the bedrock unit Soft Rock coincides with Shallow Bedrock. Softrock Hillside and Softrock Lowland provinces occur where this same rock unit coincides with Lodgment Till and Sand and Gravel, respectively.

To understand the variation in walls around the entire region, one can simply read the following descriptions of provinces. To determine which province applies to a specific property (perhaps your own), town, or county anywhere in New England, you need to determine two attributes: the type of bedrock and the type of glacial action that are present. These can be determined by locating your site of interest on the bedrock and glacial maps, using the Location Grid, which shows the location of principal cities. (For easy reference, it includes lines of latitude—42° to 47° north—and longitude—68° to 73° east—which can be found in any map atlas.) Once you know both attributes, you can read the preceding paragraphs to identify which of nine provinces your area of interest lies within, then read its description, which follows. For the Island province and the Imported province, you need consult only the surficial map, looking for the unit Moraine and the unit Fines, respectively.

For this book, I have identified eleven types of stone-wall provinces. Each is based on the type of stone dominant in the area. For convenience in description, I use the term *slab* for the schist/quartzite/slate intergrade because they almost always produce book- to briefcase-sized slabs. I have not further subdivided these provinces by cultural history.

GRANITE-GNEISS PROVINCES

Granite-gneiss intergrades, when subjected to ice-sheet glaciation, produce stones that are generally large, ranging in size and shape from typical cardboard boxes to large briefcases. These are the rocks that produce the vast majority of glacial erratics, which dot field and farm all the way from the Hampshire highlands to Nantucket. Granite, where not interbedded with gneiss, produces some of the hardest rock.

Granite block. (See photo p. 3.) When granite is near the surface, there tend to be fewer stones because many have been swept away. Additionally, the stones tend to be scarcely modified, meaning that they are jagged, and often quite irregular in shape. Rounded corners are conspicuously absent. Few productive farms were established on or near surface bedrock, which is typical of the high mountains and the Maine coast. Hence, most stone walls were arrested in the pioneering stage, or were created principally as boundary markers on estates. In the mountains, stone walls are fairly rare; if present, they tend to occur in village settings. Conversely, quarried rock is more common because hard granite is always nearby. Highland terrain did not experience the intensive farm stage, so primitive, angular walls predominate. In any case, widely spaced, jagged stones are the rule.

Granite mix. In this area the rocks tend to be severely pecked by transport in the shear zone, meaning that the corners are knocked off, especially in southern New Hampshire and upland Massachusetts. Additionally, there is a mix of pecked stone and recently entrained stone, producing great variety of stone shapes. The ablation till layer is often thinner, except near the southern coast. These are among the most characteristic stone walls of New England, in part because till is the most common surface material. There is great variety in stone size, shape, and composition. Granite quarries are also locally abundant, giving rise to a mix of quarried blocks as well. This material takes on a gray patina and a green lichen crust. (See photo p. 66.)

Granite boulder. At low elevations, stones were often buried in sand and fine gravel. In kame terrace and eskered terrain, however, walls are quite common, and built almost exclusively with stones shaped like cannonballs, watermelons, and pillows with their corners crushed off. Large angular stones are conspicuously absent. This terrain was generally more heavily settled, and thus greater attention was given to walling, often with the importation of quarried capstones. Mortar is more common as well, as it allowed some temporary control. Lexington-Concord comes to mind. The stones are often light-colored because prolonged forest clearing under sunny conditions gave rise to a powder-white patina beneath the lichen. (See photo p. 117.)

SCHIST/QUARTZITE/SLATE PROVINCES

Schist terrain is dominant over much of the New England plateau, inland from the coast but below the mountains. The area is the roughest terrain with respect to glacier action because it contains such a great variety of interbedded strong and weak rock. Most of the strong beds within schist are actually gneiss. Schist-dominated provinces are often buried with till.

Fieldstone slab. When not overlain by thick till, this rock type yields a litter of slabby stones, most of which range in size from books to briefcases. Near-surface bedrock never makes for good farm country, so the walls that do exist here are often pasture walls, which, because of the uniformly shaped stone, were easy to build. They also tend to be large walls, because on such rough country the meltout till layer was substantial. (See photo p. 136.)

Fieldstone mix. Because they are more readily crushed in the glacial mill, schists tend to produce thick till layers in which the surviving stones are pecked round, or have their corners knocked off, and the meltout till layers are often amazingly concentrated. These are the mica-rich stones that sparkle from so many walls. This terrain is the counterpoint to the granite mix, the most typical wall of New Hampshire and northern Massachusetts. Here we find the even, book-shaped walls that were so easy to build and so structurally stable that they occur all over southern New England. The thick till also gave rise to great upland farms, on which the pasture economy was based. This combination of rock type and glacial action provides a basis for the most classic well-built stone wall, composed of slabs that are hard enough to stand up to the weather, yet brittle enough to be snapped into billions of stones. Rounded stones are common, but constitute a small part of the whole, appearing often as anomalies. Because gneiss is rarer, the stones are usually darker than in walls to the north, where granite is more common. (See photo p. 1.)

Fieldstone boulder. Walls on this terrain are similar to those on granite-gneiss intergrades because it is the granite that survived. Locally, however, the esker mix and kame terraces are loaded with small quartz-rich boulders that are subrounded, with conspicuous flat joints and rounded corners. Disk-shaped boulders and cobbles are much more common than on granite-rich terrains because the corners wore away faster. Walls tend to be localized on the flanks of terraces and on eskers. These were good grain fields and mowing land, so many small stones were brought to walls as well. The pie-plate disk stone is typical. (See photo p. 133.)

SOFT-ROCK PROVINCES

Lumped into this group are the vast expanses of mudrock, including the slate of the Taconic Mountains, Vermont marble, some of the softer greenschist rocks of the Narragansett and Boston basins, and the brownstones of the Connecticut River

Valley. Ironically, the broadest expanse of soft rocks lies in Maine's north woods, in the lowland northwest of the Kahatadin Range. This would have made near perfect farmland had it not been so far from the coast and so deep into the poor soils of the evergreen forest. As a general rule, soft rocks do not produce stone walls. Where they do occur, however, the walls often contain far-traveled, odd-looking stones that had just been picked up when the glacier ice stalled in its forward motion.

Soft rock highland. Soft rock is seldom near the surface because it wasn't tough enough to stand up against the glacier. More often, it was buried by thick till. Even where scraped down to bare bones by the glacier, postglacial forests converted the rock into loamy, sandy soil. Walls are extremely rare, occurring only in unusual circumstances. There are a few places in the marble belt where the glacier left enough marble for fieldstone walls.

Soft rock hillside. The till can be very thick in areas of soft rock, especially those of southern New England. This is especially true of large drumlins, or rounded hills, of brownstone rock in the Connecticut River Valley. Some of the tills are cemented with lime, making them virtually rock hard. So few stones survived glacial crushing and postglacial weathering that fieldstone walls, if present, are very widely spaced, tumbledown, and rotting in place. This is not the case in urban areas, where rubble pits and brownstone quarries were common. Among the most curious walls of all are those made of lime-cemented till, which are rapidly falling apart. (See photo p. 175.)

Soft rock lowland. Normally, the sand and gravel of soft-rock terrain is mostly sand, smothering the stones that might have been on the surface. Where gravel predominated, however, meltwater action often flushed away much of the weak rock types, concentrating the far-traveled, more resistant visitors. Thus it is possible to find a concentration of cobbles and boulders from far-off places. Owing to this effect, this may be the only case in which walls in sand and gravel outnumber those in till. Walls are usually pathetic concentrations of cobbles and small boulders, with a high concentration of ancient quartzite, plucked, then crushed free from their soft host rocks.

Island. Technically, the moraines (accumulations of earth and stones deposited by a glacier) do not lie on granite here but on soft Cretaceous rocks. Most of the rocks on the islands were transported by glacier from the north, however, and were strong enough to survive the trip. Moraine walls have the most worn-down rocks of all, and thus are characterized by the most resistant types and shapes. Basically, granite alone could survive a trip that involved not only grinding at the base of the ice but also tumbling in subglacial streams. The result is generally subrounded material concentrated in distinct patches; some thrust ridges contained boulders, whereas others were dominated by rafts of sand. The moraines for all the hills and high ground of Nantucket, Martha's Vineyard, the Lower Cape (Cod), the Elizabeth Islands, the Charlestown area of mainland Rhode Island, Block Island, and the North and South Forks of Long Island as well as its main stem are in areas that were settled early and farmed intensively, usually in association with a mercantile economy. The islands provided perfect opportunities for intensive grazing, and the generally sandy soils ensured that plenty of rocks were produced. The islands were also centers of later wealth. Hence, the mix of wall style and form is quite variable. As a general rule, however, the combination of concentrated farms, money, and equant, sun-bleached stone allowed significant effort with subangular to subrounded stones where sheep pasture was common. The end result was the lace wall so typical of the islands. Mortared cobblestone walls, on the other hand, reflect Victorian-era tourism. (See photo p. 134.)

Imported. Fieldstone is virtually absent in places where broad glacial lakes existed. This is particularly true in the Hudson River valley-Lake Champlain Lowland, and the Connecticut River and Merrimack River valleys. It is also true along the Gulf of Maine, especially north of Rockport, Massachusetts, where the stones are buried by mud deposited in the sea as the ice sheet withdrew. In places where granite is nearby, stone walls are common even in areas without surface stone, as this rock type was so easily quarried. These conditions span an enormous area north of Boston, the Acadian rocks along the coast of Rockport, the sliver of New Hampshire coast, and a giant wedge inland from the coast of Maine, reaching its farthest point near Farmington. Walls occur only in settled regions. (See top photo p. 21.)

EXCEPTIONS

There are some flagrant, and amazing, exceptions to the mapping conventions used above. Most prominent is the traprock wall, which is composed almost entirely of basalt. The Palisades of the Hudson River, East and West Rock in New Haven, the Holyoke Range, and the elongate ridges throughout the Connecticut River Valley are made of completely unmetamorphosed basalt, either cooled lava flows or the dikes and sills that fed them. This rock is hard, prominent, and forms columns. There is no classification type because, although locally important, basalt does not crop out over areas broad enough to map at the scale of a province.

Another important exception is the presence of hard-rock anomalies within the marble belt. When unmodified, marble is among the softest rocks, hardly capable of producing stone walls. When penetrated by fluids rich in magnesium and silicon, however, marble can become almost as strong as quartzite. One great thing about these boulders is their odd shapes, which mimic the zones of fluid replacement.

Sometimes granite is exceptionally weak, especially if its micas were altered to clay by hydrothermal fluids, or because the crystals are huge, as they are in pegmatites. In such circumstances a stone can consist of a single crystal, rather than an aggregate of them.

SUBREGIONS

Though New England is a single region, it can be broken down into seven distinct subregions, based on its stone walls. North Woods; Gulf of Maine; White Mountains; Green Mountains; Southwest Highlands; Southeast Hills; and Sandy Coast. Few stone walls are present in the North Walls of New England, which takes in the Northeast Kingdom of Vermont, much of Coos County in New Hampshire, and most of northwestern Maine above Rangeley Lakes. Pasture and tillage agriculture were never as dominant there as forestry and wilderness activities such as fishing, hunting, and canoeing. Much of the area is also underlain by soft rocks.

Fieldstone walls along the Gulf of Maine coast (which begins north of Gloucester, Massachusetts) lie only above the level of the postglacial sea, which covered almost all fairly low-rolling country with flat sheets of mud. South of the head of Casco Bay (from Bath to Brunswick, Maine) historic walls on lowland marshes, sand plains, and broad river lowlands are, thus, very rare. Yet, they are nearly ubiquitous on the till-smeared hills that once stood as islands above the ancient sea, places that were peppered with dairy farms. Farther Down East, especially east of Penobscot Bay (Maine's largest), agricultural walls become more rare and less massive because the economy focused on fishing and timbering, then tourism. There, seaside walls are typically composed of quarried stone and are associated with port construction and summer residences.

New Hampshire's White Mountains (and related highlands of southwestern Maine) are the highest, most rugged part of New England. Walls here are almost overwhelmingly composed of granite, bleached to a light gray color, and covered with lichens. In the highlands, the walls are massive, widely spaced, and built principally of slabs and blocks. In lowlands, the walls are also massive, but usually built of boulders dominated by large two-handers and assisted stones. Buildings and transportation works are often built of quarried granite, owing to the ubiquity and quality of this rock.

Vermont's stone walls reflect the abrupt contrasts between the hard ancient rocks of the Green Mountains, and the softer rocks of the hills and lowlands. Lowland walls are typically absent because the land was either buried with sandy mud or the rocks were too weak. The same is true for the high country, which was too rugged for most farming activities. In the middle ground between valleys and summits, however, much of the country was given over to grazing by sheep and dairy cows. Stone walls there are seldom either massive or concentrated. Instead, they are usually fairly nondescript, except for the relatively high frequency of quartz boulders.

The Southwestern Highlands include the Litchfield Hills and Berkshire Mountains in Connecticut and Massachusetts, respectively, and the Taconic Mountains in New York, especially toward the south. None of it is truly mountainous, but most of it is till-smeared highland. Settlement was late, and never that intensive. Stone walls are widely distributed and typically restricted to village centers and boundary walls on landholdings. Walls are more concentrated and well built as they get closer to the Hudson and Connecticut rivers, respectively.

The Southeastern Hills include eastern Massachusetts (exclusive of its coastal plain), eastern Connecticut, and all of Rhode Island. In this subregion, the combination of slabby rock and strong glacial action produced a high concentration of slabby fieldstones over most of the inland areas, making it the epicenter of the classic farmstead wall. Granite predominates only near the coast.

Historic walls of the Sandy Coast (Cape Cod to Staten Island, including the islands) are present only on the moraine ridges. Most of the original farm walls were used to divide property where sheep were grazed, the sandy soils not being suited for cereal crops. Walls today are generally massive, well-built property walls that enhance expensive residential and tourist properties. Stone architecture in the towns and villages is usually a mix of imported quarried stone and mortared cobblestone decorations.

CHAPTER 11

WALLS TO VISIT

For twenty years, my family and I have traveled to typical New England destinations: the mountains of New Hampshire, valleys in Vermont, the Maine coast, Newport's mansions, and Boston. My middle son's frame of reference for each trip is the food he had there. While teasing him about this one day, my wife reminded me that that is exactly what I do with stone walls. She's right. I can still recall the stone walls at Clara Barton's birthplace, Herman Melville's home, Thoreau's Walden, and Edith Wharton's Gilded Age property, though I can't recall the layout of the rooms or even the name of the last.

This chapter is essentially a tour guide to New England stone walls, including stone walls within and near the most visited tourist destinations. Then, for the more serious stone-wall enthusiast, I offer a list of walls special enough to be destinations in and of themselves.

TOURIST WALLS

Walls are present near most popular New England tourist destinations. Learning more about the walls near a destination can add enjoyment to the main attraction. Furthermore the association between each destination and a stone wall province can help you understand the regional distribution of stone walls. The information that follows is organized by tourist sites arranged by state from north to south, beginning with Maine and ending with New York.

MAINE

ACADIA NATIONAL PARK

Granite block

Located near Bar Harbor, Acadia is the most visited national park in the Northeast. Soil is thin to nonexistent. This area is so glacially scoured that even the resistant rock ridges have been carved into streamlined shapes, Cadillac Mountain being the most famous. Expertly laid granite quarrystone walls in the bridges and trails are common, laid down at a time when this was a playground for the rich during the Gilded Age. Fieldstone walls are generally rare, owing to the dearth of surface stone. Where present, they are small and rubbly. Stone cairns are common on the trails.

LAKES DISTRICT

Fieldstone mix

In Kennebec and Androscoggin counties, thousands of long lakes were scoured into the bedrock grain by the passage of the ice. The Belgrade Lakes and Auburn Lake are two examples. Had this area been on the coast, the lakes would be indented fjords. The deepest scouring took place in belts of metamorphic rock that were strong, but less so than the adjacent granite highlands. There is much granite around, but less so than on surrounding terrain. Many of the boulders have the beaten-up look typical of Maine's lumpy stones, bruised within the till. Stone towers and odd forms are often present.

Gulf of Maine: large granite boulders, Bar Harbor/ Acadia, Maine

MOUNT KATAHDIN

Granite block

Mount Katahdin, at 5,268 feet above sea level, is twelve feet short of a mile high, and the first place in the United States to be lit by sunrise. It is a wilderness peak, carved from granite by alpine glaciers, which formed its famous knife edge, not by the invading ice sheet from the north. There are no stone walls high up on Mount Katahdin that result from agricultural and farming ac-

Lakes District, Maine: a well cover at Sabbathday Lake Village

tivity because this has always been wild country. A few walls and cairns are present in Baxter State Park, which protects Maine's highest peak and the surrounding area from development. Where present, walls are slabs of granite, just barely arranged.

YORK-PORTLAND

Granite boulder

Maine's largest beaches lie in this zone, between Portland to the north and York Beach to the south. Included here is the honky-tonk waterfront of Old Orchard Beach, Kennebunkport, and the upscale summer residence Ogunquit. The beaches are here because this southern fringe of the Gulf of Maine was submerged by the sea as the glacier withdrew, leaving sandy marine mud to the east and sand and gravel to the west. Most of the terrain is flat, with stony hills rising above the flat, stone-free lowlands. Walls are present in most upland areas. Built from the granite to the west in the vicinity of Lake Sebago, they are largely composed of water-worn boulders. The striking thing about this country is the ubiquity of walls above the flatlands and (except for quarried rock) their virtual absence below. (See photo p. 3.)

NEW HAMPSHIRE

LAKE WINNEPESAUKE

Granite mix

New Hampshire's largest lake is aligned with the ice-flow direction. The glacial scouring that carved the lake also crushed many of the boulders into sand, which was plastered over the surface as a layer of sandy till. Stone walls are almost exclusively made of light-colored granite, usually of blocks with their corners and edges pecked away. Much of this was good pastureland, especially for sheep, before it became a tourist mecca dominated by boating. Still, it's granite, granite, granite nearly everywhere, principally in potato-shaped, watermelon-sized lumps. (See photo p. 78.)

MOUNT MONADNOCK

Granite block

Mount Monadnock is the upland counterpart to Lake Winnepesauke, and the peak climbed so often by Henry David Thoreau. Both are made of granite, but the mountain is convex to the sky, whereas the lake is concave. Its bald top, just barely above the tree line, is littered with windswept granite slabs only partly covered by lichens, tenacious willows, and conifers. Thousands of people climb this peak each year. Stone walls are common on the lower slopes, which were extensively used for grazing sheep. There are also large boundary walls built to demarcate large landholdings. The higher the wall is, the more likely it is to be composed of large blocky shapes. The lower one goes, the more likely the walls are to be built from subrounded stones. (See photo p. 113.)

Lake Winnepesauke, New Hampshire: a boulder wall near Center Harbor

North Conway

Granite block

North Conway is the gateway to the White Mountains from the southeast, the direction from which most tourists come. It lies in a broad, flaring glacially scoured trough. Stone walls are more common as part of the development of the resort industry in the late nineteenth century than from agriculture. They were built usually for architectural purposes, and usually in the middle ground—neither high up, where rock rubble dominates, nor far down in the valley bottoms, where sand and gravel dominate. The chief value of North Conway country for the stone-wall enthusiast is that it lies within striking distance of enough granite to build a wall around the whole state of New Hampshire, which takes its nickname from the rock itself.

Vermont

Breadloaf-Middlebury

Fieldstone slab

Breadloaf is nestled in a small valley cut into the eastern slope of the Green Mountains. Robert Frost, who worked and taught at nearby Middlebury College, lived there on and off, using the landscape for inspiration. Now a nationally known writers' conference takes place every year. Stone walls are generally rare, except on broad upland summits where sheep grazed by the thousands, and near the base of the valleys just above streams. There is a mixture of material here, because the mountains are composed of different layers thrust up on edge. (See photo p. 73.)

Manchester

Fieldstone slab

Manchester is the main tourist center in southwestern Vermont, especially for those who come by the busloads to see the annual display of fall foliage. The village lies in a narrow valley where the marble had been dissolved away, even before the glacier came and crushed what was left. The narrow lowland contin-

Stone-free soil in the Lake Champlain Lowland in Vermont

ues south to Connecticut and north to the Canadian border. To the east are highlands, rising to Stratton Mountain, an important ski destination for western New England. On the slopes midway between valleys and ridges are many stone walls, though not nearly as concentrated as to the south. They are built of large, generally dark slabs of fairly undistinguished rock, often peppered with quartz boulders. (I call them dalmatian walls.) (See top photo p. 52.)

SHELBURNE FALLS

Imported

Lake Champlain is a residue of a once much larger glacial lake into which settled billions of tons of mud. This smothered the stones and created some of the finest agricultural soil for New England crops. The northern part of the basin was even invaded by the sea before the land rose back up again, its glacial weight removed. The area's principal city, Burlington, was built on a large sand and gravel delta that once fed into the lake. Stone walls are very rare over most of the terrain, except on small islands that once poked above the floor of the old lake bed. Shelburne typifies this landscape in the heart of the glacial lake, where stone walls are imported.

MASSACHUSETTS

BERKSHIRES

Granite mix

The Berkshires in Massachusetts are a range of low mountains held up by a lozenge-shaped mass of granite within the surrounding sea of weaker rocks. They are gentle mountains rather than rigorous ones. All of the summits are below the tree line, and the scenery is one of pleasant vistas of meadows and woodland. Stone walls seem to be either slabs in sprawling pastures or bouldery fences in the more narrow valleys, where the stones are concentrated. Ornate stone walls are especially common on the many estates within the region especially near Tanglewood in Lennox, summer home of the Boston symphony orchestra.

CHATHAM, CAPE COD

Island

Chatham, a picturesque historic whaling/fishing village, lies at the elbow of the Cape. The forearm and closed fist are the outer cape and Provincetown, respectively, home to Cape Cod National Seashore. The inner arm of the cape lies between Chatham and the Cape Cod Canal. The digging for the canal was fairly easy because most of the region is underlain by glacially washed sand. Its walls are mostly made of rounded boulders and cobblestones. These last are particularly prominent in the village center, where they are mortared into retaining

Typical roadside wall in the Berkshires in Massachusetts

Mortared cobblestones in the Victorian style, Chatham Village, Massachusetts

walls, pedestals, and archways with Victorian motifs. Many of the cobbles were obtained from the beach, rather than from the fields. The few stone walls in Chatham built of boulders used fieldstones that survived glacial transport from the north, now submerged beneath the sea.

LEXINGTON-CONCORD

Granite boulder

Concord was the place where the "shot heard round the world" that started the American War of Independence was fired. It was here that a militia of minutemen fired across the old North Bridge, returning British fire. It was also here that Ralph Waldo Emerson, Henry David Thoreau, Nathaniel Hawthorne, and Louisa May Alcott took inspiration from the areas' meadows and marshes, glacial drumlins, and kettle ponds, of which Walden Pond is the most famous. Located inland only ten to fifteen miles from Boston, this was one of the few inland areas densely settled by the time of the American Revolution. Early settlement was due to the expanse of stone-free lowland soils located at the confluence of the Sudbury and Concord rivers, soils that formed at the bottom of an earlier glacial lake. The combination of early settlement, abundant rounded boulders, and otherwise fine agricultural soils have led to a concentration of stone walls, many of which are fairly tall fences. These line much of the length of the Battle Road, now part of Minuteman National Park. (See photo p. 150.)

Martha's Vineyard

Island

Chilmark, Martha's Vineyard, is famous for its stone walls, especially for its lace walls. With real estate prices so high and free time so plentiful, thousands of stone walls are being rebuilt across the island. Martha's Vineyard is shaped like a triangle. Its northern apex is where two terminal moraines come together. The eastern one swings to the southeast in a broad arc that outlines the former margin of a former glacial lobe, one that came through Cape Cod Bay. The western side is similar, but marks the margin of a lobe that came down Buzzards Bay. The rest of the island is sand. One of the curious things about Vineyard walls is that they are restricted to the moraines, generally to their northern sides.

Old Sturbridge Village

Fieldstone mix

Old Sturbridge Village is a living history museum, where some of the exhibits are people walking around in traditional garb, reenacting the way things were done in the early nineteenth century. They even build stone walls for the visitors to see. Sturbridge lies in a belt of rock that extends all the way from Long Island Sound near Branford and Guilford, Connecticut, through the hills of eastern Connecticut, across all of Massachusetts, and all the way to near Concord, New Hampshire. This is dominantly a mixture of schist and gneisses, with quite a bit of slate and dull mudrock thrown in for good measure. These stones are generally slabby rather than blocky. The hills are almost all covered with glacial till, which was excellent pasture. In this swath of terrain lies the agricultural heartland of New England, and the epicenter of its stone walls, at least those of prosperous farms. (See photo p. 136.)

Plymouth Colony

Granite boulder

Plymouth is home to Plymouth Rock, America's most famous boulder. This isolated granite boulder, a glacial erratic, is alleged to have protruded through the sand when the Pilgrims landed in 1620, as if it were a beacon guiding them to shore. The boulder itself, now caged behind bars, looks more like a stepped-on potato. The bay for Plymouth lies at the boundary between ancient hard rocks to the north and the broad expanse of coastal-plain soft rocks to the south. Hence, the walls of the vicinity vary. Those in the village itself are usually of granite quarried from northerly sources. Those to the south are fairly rare, and consist only of rounded boulders.

CONNECTICUT

Southeastern Hills: well-laid fieldstone walls, Woodstock, Connecticut

LITCHFIELD HILLS

Fieldstone mix

Litchfield is an iconic village, a group of prominent hills, and a county in the heart of northwestern Connecticut. Formerly a thriving agricultural landscape, it is now home to the wealthy with New York connections. Similar to the Berkshires to the north and the Taconics to the west, it is a till-covered rolling landscape. The walls are typically blocky in form, usually double and well built, composed of a mixture of granite, mudrock, and slabby rocks.

MYSTIC SEAPORT

Granite mix

Mystic, home to an important whaling fleet in the nineteenth century, has been a center of maritime commerce since early colonial times. Mystic Village is Connecticut's most visited tourist attraction. The seaport itself contains hundreds of examples of walls built of quarried granite slabs, cut from nearby sources, which are abundant, and fitted with the bolts for ropes and chains so typical of shipyard wharves and piers. Yet five miles to the north, in Old Mystic and nearby Stonington, one can find primitive farmstead walls in great abundance. Almost always they are blocky, consisting of an equal mixture of glacially pecked granite chunks, a few well-rounded cobbles, and the occasional slab or two. Early village walls were used for curbing, wharves, piers, and mills.

Quarried granite below a wooden fence, Mystic Seaport, Connecticut

RHODE ISLAND

NEWPORT

Fieldstone mix

Narragansett Bay was no glacial accident. It was scoured deeply because it lies above a geological basin, the Narragansett Basin, which contains younger and softer rocks than those on either side of the bay. Most of this younger rock is composed of gray, slatelike stone with a green hue, but there is also an abundance of puddingstone, more so than anywhere else in New England. There are three basic types of stone walls in Newport and its surroundings. Most common are those in the adjacent rural towns, especially little Compton, many of which are now parts of sprawling equestrian farms and land-rich, house-poor estates. Second in prominence are the many high, very well built estate walls that surround the "cottages" of the wealthy—actually large mansions guarded by high stone walls, many of them capped with sharp copestones or iron spikes. Easiest to see are those along the famous Cliff Walk,

a public pedestrian path that follows the top of the cliff, between the sea below and the many mansions above. Most of the walls there were built by skilled masons, over many stages of construction. Sea walls, facing walls, turrets, and towers are all freely visible to the thousands of tourists who come to explore the magnificent summer scenery of Newport.

Sandy Coast: modern pasture fences,
Block Island, Rhode Island

New York

The Hamptons

Island

The Hamptons is a concentration of old towns on the South Fork of Long Island, New York—Southampton, Easthampton, Hampton Bays, and West Hampton. Famous for its Atlantic beaches, the area beckons seasonal tourists and many wealthy year-round residents with New York City connections. The towns are sited on sand plains and marsh estuaries that front the moraine that forms the South Fork. Stone walls come in two basic forms. Many in the village centers were built of imported stone, owing to the concentration of wealth and shoreline access. To the north, walls are generally absent because even the moraines are overwhelmingly sandy. Where present, however, they are generally small and consist of durable boulders (generally granite) that were carried across what is now Long Island Sound and dumped by the glaciers at its southern limit.

Hudson Valley

Fieldstone mix

The Hudson Valley forms a broad gorge north of New York City, cutting against the grain through several strong geological units. Above Poughkeepsie, however, the river is aligned with the grain of the land, having found the seam between New England and what used to be the eastern edge of North America. From Poughkeepsie to Albany, the eastern, New England, part of the valley consists of elevation zones from the Taconic Mountains, to foothills, to abandoned glacial lake shorelines, to river-cut terraces, to floodplains, then finally to the water itself. This was early, productive, settled agricultural land. Stone walls abound, especially to the east, especially in Westchester, Putnam, and Dutchess counties. The rock is slabby, rather than granite. Walls are concentrated in the lower foothills and just above the river terraces. (See photo p. 36.)

New York City

Fieldstone slab

New York City sprawls over terrain that lay just above the terminal zone of the last glacial advance. Hence boulders are common, as are zones of intensely scoured rock. Stone walls in the area tell a story of quarrying, heavy industry, immigrant labor, and urban architecture. Rock from around the world has been brought to New York for the exteriors and interiors of its buildings. Urban air pollution is contributing to deterioration of the walls, especially those mortared with concrete.

NOTEWORTHY WALLS

Some walls are worth a special visit, especially if you live nearby, or if you have taken up stone-wall watching as a serious hobby. Clearly everyone, expert and nonexpert alike, will have their own list of favorite walls, just as they have their favorite restaurants or swimming holes. Below is my idiosyncratic list of twenty-four favorites, organized into five different categories. A quirky list, derived from my own bias, travels, and investigations, it also reflects a compromise between the walls I know best, those that are easily accessible, and those distributed throughout the region. Six walls are notable for the rock composition of their stones. Four are listed because of their size or form. Five illustrate geographic limits or are especially characteristic of a geographic region; and finally, nine are included due to my own value judgments. Many readers may know of wider, taller, or more massive walls, for I have no doubt that they exist. If so, please contact me through the Stone Wall Initiative Web site.

ROCK TYPE

GEMS AND CRYSTALS

Perham's of Maine, West Paris, Maine. Located at the intersection of State Highways 219 and 26.

An old rock shop and jewelry store in the heart of Maine's pegmatite mining district. At the entrance is a mortared wall containing dozens of crystals, agates, and visually striking rocks, many from nearby sources. In the shop are maps for self-guided tours to quarries for gem prospectors of all ages. (See photo p. 27.)

Green Mountains: soft slate and limestone, Crown Point, New York

LIMESTONE

Chimney Point/Crown Point, Vermont/New York. The site can be reached by either Vermont State Highway 17 or Vermont State Highway 125. (There is an admission fee for access to the fort on the New York side.)

Lying across the western boundary of New England is an area too far northwest to have been metamorphosed into marble. These gray, laminated, marine sedimentary rocks are full of early Paleozoic fossils that can be seen most easily in the stone walls of the derelict fort on the New York side. They were deposited on the continental shelf when this edge of North America had a tropical, equatorial climate.

SANDSTONE

West Hartford, Connecticut. Located just west of its eastern border with Hartford. On private property on the north side of the intersection of Albany Avenue and Prospect Street, but clearly visible from the sidewalk.

This ornate estate wall is built of red Jurassic sandstone with a mortared top. Visible on the street side of the wall are ripple marks, raindrop impressions, mud cracks, cross beds, pebble horizons, and various tool marks. The best way to see the wall is from the public sidewalk at the crosswalk. (See photo p. 37.)

BASALT

Hill-Stead Museum, Farmington, Connecticut. Located just south of the intersection of Connecticut State Highways 10 and 4. Follow official brown signs, turning east opposite Miss Porter's School. (No admission fee required to see the walls.)

Pure basaltic traprock at the Hill-Stead Museum in Connecticut

A world-renowned collection of American Impressionist paintings can be found at this lovely Colonial Revival mansion on a traprock ridge overlooking the Farmington Valley. This is also the site of the very popular annual Sunken Garden poetry festival. Walls on the estate, particularly those paralleling the long entry, are built almost entirely of black basalt boulders taken from the property as well as imported from railroad blasting debris.

GRANITE

Roadside Walls, Stonington, Connecticut. Located by taking Exit 91 off Interstate 91 and heading either west (toward Old Mystic) or east (toward Pawcatuck) on State Highway 234.

This is an old road with its roadside walls rebuilt almost exclusively with Avalonian granite blocks. There is a mix of laid and stacked walls. Walls are more concentrated on the eastern side.

MIXED LITHOLOGY

Orient, Long Island, New York. Located by heading west on New York State Highway 25 from the Orient Point ferry terminal into Orient Village, then to Greenport. Walls occur here and there on the north side of the road, adjacent to the public sidewalk.

In several spots the walls contain a widely varied mix of material; fieldstone boulders of quartzite, granite, and metamorphic rock; blast rubble of granite, probably hauled from urban demolition; cobble-sized lumps of brick, asphalt, and cement. Some of the stones may have come from more than a thousand miles away. (See photo p. 40.)

SIZE AND FORM

THE TALLEST WALL

Cliff Walk, Newport, Rhode Island. Located in the city of Newport just below Bellevue Avenue mansions and above the rocky shore south of Easton Beach, off Rhode Island State Highway 138A. The wall is approximately one-quarter mile in from the parking area.

Cliff Walk offers spectacular views of Narragansett Bay from a safe, public paved trail, accessible from several points. Many different kinds of stonework are visible. One of the seawalls protecting the shore from erosion is the tallest one I have seen. I estimate it at more than 100 feet high. (See photo p. 58.)

THE WIDEST WALL

Spring Hill, Connecticut. Located by following Spring Hill Road west from State Highway 195 in the historic district of Mansfield, Connecticut, just opposite the historical museum. Approximately two-thirds of a mile west, just beyond the crossing of a natural gas pipeline and on the south side of the road, is a broad wall more than twenty feet wide in some places.

I have seen similar walls that are not only wider but better built, but they were on restricted government land. I have also heard tall tales of even wider walls.

A BOULDERY WALL

Center Harbor Area, New Hampshire. Located on municipal and private property visible from New Hampshire State Highway 25 and along Bean Road in Center Harbor.

Walls in this vicinity are built of massive potato-shaped granite boulders, sometimes averaging about three feet in intermediate diameter. Smaller stones are absent in some places. (See photo p. 130.)

A Massive Wall

New Croton Reservoir, New York. The reservoir crosses State Highway 129 just east of Croton-on-Hudson, Westchester County, New York.

This massive wall was built almost completely around the reservoir in the 1890s by immigrant (mostly Italian) labor to protect it from water contamination, especially by grazing cattle. More than a century has elapsed, yet the wall stands strong and firm.

Geography

The Most Uniform Distribution

Little Compton, Rhode Island. Located along both sides of the road along State Highway 77 between Tiverton and Sakonnet Point and on many (if not all) subsidiary roads.

Stone walls of a similar style, built of the local low-grade, generally gray, metamorphic stone, are continuously present along the roadside, along with hundreds of perpendicular walls that junction from them. Though I have seen more concentrated walls, I have never seen such a concentration over so broad an area. (See photo p. 62.)

The Sharpest Northern Limit

Weld Corner, Maine. Located on State Highway 142 north of Weld, Maine, in Franklin County.

The small village of Weld Corner has a variety of large granite-block stone walls. Driving north from Weld Corner along Route 142, I was struck by the abrupt termination of the roadside stone walls. I continued to drive north to State Highway 4, then west to Rangely and beyond, seeing hardly any stone walls at all. Certainly there are walls farther north, but never have I seen the

presence/absence boundary so sharply ex-
pressed by latitude.

THE BEST-PRESERVED WALL PATTERN

Harvard Forest, Petersham, Massachusetts.
Located northeast of Quabbin Reservoir in
lands marked "Harvard Forest" along State
Highways 122 and 32A. The walls are on
the private property of Harvard University;
visible from local roads. (Permission is
required to enter.)

Much of Petersham was abandoned as an
agricultural district in the mid-eighteenth
century. Harvard University purchased the
land, which it later converted into a forestry
research station, now a world-class ecosystem
study area. Because the land was purchased
early and left unchanged, the pattern of walls
is preserved more or less intact. Research into
the impact of stone walls on forest ecosystems
is taking place here.

*North Woods: Fenceline rubble from
the pioneering stage, Weld, Maine*

THE OLDEST WALL

Popham Point, Sagadohoc, Maine. Popham Beach State Park and an
abandoned fort are located off State Highway 209 south of Bath, Maine.

The oldest known documentary mention of a stone wall in New England is
of this one. In 1607 the North Virginia Company established a colony with
the intent of permanent settlement. Though it disappeared within the year, a
letter cited by the historian Howard Russell strongly suggests that the
colonists built a stone wall, which was later destroyed or buried.

A Hidden Wall

Tinkhamtown, Lyme, New Hampshire. Located somewhere in the woods east of the Appalachian Trail past the Dartmouth ski facility below Winslow Ledge. (I won't say exactly where.)

Though one is identified on the official U.S. Geological Survey Maps, there never really was a town here. Rather, it was an isolated farmstead in the foothills of the White Mountains dating to the early nineteenth century, then thoroughly overgrown. An old cemetery associated with the farmstead couldn't be located for decades after it was last witnessed in the 1950s, in spite of many attempts. It was recently rediscovered.

Value Judgments

The Most Famous Wall

Frost's mending wall, Derry, New Hampshire. Located on state Highway 28, approximately one mile south of its intersection with Highway 280P in Rockingham County. (Admission fee required.)

On this site is a private museum exhibiting the poet Robert Frost's life, especially on this farm. Located just behind the house is the mending wall,

the namesake for the most famous poem about stone walls, which begins, "Something there is that doesn't love a wall. . . ."

Robert Frost's mending wall, Derry, New Hampshire

The Saddest Wall

South Eagleville Road, Storrs, Connecticut. Located on the boundary between private property and the right-of-way along State Highway 275, between State Highways 32 and 195, directly opposite the entrance to a senior housing complex.

This wall is literally dissolving. Its stones are composed of a schist that contains an abundance of metal sulfide minerals that quickly rust when exposed to rain, liberating sulfuric acid in the process. Many of the stones, probably placed no more than a few decades ago, have completely turned to powder, which washes away. One day I expect the wall's skeleton to fall down completely.

A Humbled Wall

Acadia National Park, Bar Harbor, Maine. Located on the east side of Mount Desert Island, right side of the road, near the first overlook.

This road has several small rubble walls that pre-date the grand stonework of the Gilded Age. The contrast between the two makes for the most dramatic historical juxtaposition I am aware of. (See photo p. 82.)

The Most Out-of-Place Wall

Dixville Notch, New Hampshire. Located on the access road entering Balsams Wilderness Resort, off State Highway 26.

The local rock is a highly foliated, weak schist that produces landslides in the notch. This wall rock, probably left over from road con-struction, was used to build a high, carefully laid copestone wall in the ornate style, similar to what one might find surrounding Anglican churches in colonial Newport, Rhode Island.

Ornate copestones looking somewhat out of place at Dixville Notch, New Hampshire

The combination of the estate look, the weak rock, and it far-north location in New Hampshire make it seem otherworldly.

The Oddest Wall

Stone Pale Wall, Hingham, Massachusetts. The Trustees of Reservations, a land trust operating throughout Massachusetts, maintains a property for public use in Hingham called World's End. Located on the east side of the street and just south of the property access is a series of unusual stone walls.

Large, blade-shaped stones, both natural and quarried, have been inserted into the ground. Each would be considered a standing stone had they not been abutted together, forming a wall that looks like a row of wide Popsicle sticks, rammed into the ground.

A Wannabe Wall

Newport mansions, Newport, Rhode Island. Many of the mansions in Newport are surrounded by high estate walls, especially along the east–west connecting roads (Sea View Avenue, Narragansett Avenue, Webster Street, and Leroy Avenue) between Cliff Walk and Bellevue Avenue.

Several of the walls here are made of granite blocks that are precisely cut and fitted into unusual arrangements that resemble those of the Incan stonework at Machu Picchu, in Peru.

An Indian Wall

Mashantucket Pequot Museum and Research Center, Mashantucket Pequot Reservation, Ledyard, Connecticut. This public museum is located on tribal property just off State Highway 2, which runs directly behind the northern side of the building.

At the landscaped rear of the building is a fine example of the Narragansett style of wall building; its construction was contracted to Narragansett masons, who have worked in this area continuously during the last several generations.

AN UNUSUAL WALL

America's Stonehenge, North Salem, New Hampshire. Located on State Highway 111, about two miles north of its intersection with State Highway 28. (Admission fee required.)

There is some really odd and fascinating stonework here. Waste rock from an old quarry was moved about to create chambers and passageways, and placed in excavations to form a circle of standing stones, alleged to

Odd stonework at "America's Stonehenge," North Salem, New Hampshire

be an astronomical observatory. Other stones are claimed to be altars, sacrificial tables, and so forth. What was originally dubbed "Mystery Hill" by early antiquarians was later bought as an attraction and renamed "America's Stonehenge" to ensure the flow of gullible tourists.

AN IMPORTANT WALL

The Old Manse, Concord, Massachusetts. Concord Center is located on State Highway 62. From there, take Monument Street north to the turnoff for the Old North Bridge. The Old Manse is the house across the street, clearly marked with a sign placed by the Trustees of Reservations.

The Old Manse is the name given to this old gray clapboard house by Nathaniel Hawthorne, who lived there in the early 1840s. The house was built by the Reverend William Emerson, who, looking out the window—almost certainly over the stone wall that marks the edge of the house lot—was able to witness the hostilities between the British regulars and the Minutemen. In 1834 his grandson, Ralph Waldo Emerson, began writing his first published

essay, *Nature,* there. I would like to think that the old granite-boulder wall seen from the window gave inspiration to Emerson, sage of the Transcendentalist movement, which led to a rethinking of the relationship between man and nature.

View of the Old North Bridge from the Old Manse, Concord, Massachusetts

EPILOGUE:
STONE WALLS AND THE ECOSYSTEM

Try to imagine the old-growth forest that once covered New England's hills and valleys before the Europeans arrived in the seventeenth century—enormous cathedral pines, stately chestnuts, hemlock groves. At the time there were no stone walls in the deep woods. Since then, the original vegetation has been cleared, up to 250,000 miles of stone wall have been built, much of the farmland has been abandoned, and the woods have regrown. Over time, and for better or worse, stone walls and local ecosystems have become part of a unified system. They influence each other.

If all of these stone walls—probably more than 100,000 miles of them—vanished today, a surge of physical and biological changes would ripple through the landscape. Patches of woodland formerly kept apart by the stone would blend together. Without the walls, billions of creatures—those that require its stony habitat—would die. Others would move to remaining ledges where they would compete for territory. Chain die-offs between predator, prey, and scavenger would occur. For example, when millions of chipmunks and field mice are gone for good, which predators will be affected? Without the walls, what are now shaded cold spots and sunny warm spots would disappear. Without walls the woods would remain a mosaic of microhabitats governed by slope, shade, and moisture, but to a lesser extent than before. No longer would the tops of walls resemble the habitat of rocky deserts, their bases the moist caves of humid regions.

The physical landscape would adjust as well. Billions of truckloads of sediment, formerly trapped on the uphill sides of stone walls on gentle slopes, would wash downward to streams. Trout would take notice. Thousands of wetlands would drain away, the source of their impoundment removed. Turtles would lose their homes. Small streams held in check by stone walls would revert back to their old

Four separate microclimates on walls flanking streams, eastern Connecticut

channels, now that the confinement was gone. The pools and riffles of countless small brooks created by the abutments for old stone bridges would disappear, the streams becoming straighter, simpler, and less interesting. Floodplains would be more heavily scoured during peak flow, as the walls built across them would no longer calm the waters and hold back the sediment. No longer would walls act like cracks to let water leak into the soil during rains, then wick it out during dry spells. No longer would they pump heat into and out of the ground to make hot and cold spots in the soil.

Walls also influence the local wind, especially along the coast or on ridges, where there is a prevailing windward and leeward side of each wall. The windward side is colder for a north wind, and warmer for a south wind, vice versa for the leeward side, amplifying the effect of shade and sun. Sometimes the combined effects of sun and wind are indirect, operating through the presence or absence of snow accumulation and melting. Snow lingers longer on the north side of the wall, increasing moisture and delaying spring, sometimes for weeks. More rain is caught on the side from which rainstorms blow.

Collapse of a wall culvert, causing the impoundment of a brook, eastern Connecticut

Beyond the influence of walls on snow, rain, wind, and shade is the influence of walls on soil erosion. On all forested and grassy slopes, there is a slow, but imperceptible movement of the soil in a downhill direction. This process, called soil creep, is especially important in the top foot of the soil, declining in importance with depth. A wall always catches the creeping soil on the uphill side, causing a buildup of soil there and a net loss of soil on the downhill side. In some circumstances, the weight and lateral pressure of the soil trapped on the uphill side combines with the loss of soil support on the downhill side to push the wall over. Walls strong enough to survive develop a wedge of creeping sediment on the uphill side, one that feathers into the slope about ten to twenty feet higher. The wedge is invariably drier than the surrounding soils, because it is raised above the water table and because the fines have been selectively washed downward. Flowers grow there that cannot grow elsewhere.

New England is a place where human activities are so thoroughly blended into the otherwise natural landscape that the distinction between them is moot and meaningless. Stone walls are the most important, most visible part of this impact. They link historic sites into a heritage landscape. They link habitats into an ecological mosaic. They allow the history to be linked to the ecology, creating a landscape in which history and natural history are one in the same. To thoughtlessly strip-mine stone walls from such a landscape, to sell them as if they were so much blast rubble, is to unravel the binding threads that hold our patchwork landscape of culture and nature together.

APPENDIX

Maps
Additional Resources
Tools and Equipment
Classification Key
Life List of Walls

Location Grid

0   50
Miles

Caribou

Greenville

Newport

VERMONT

Burlington

Rangeley

Bangor

MAINE

Gorham

Montpelier

Fryeburg

Machias

Rutland

Hanover

Concord

Portland

NEW
HAMPSHIRE

Brattleboro

Portsmouth

Albany

Pittsfield

Nashua

MASSACHUSETTS

NEW
YORK

Springfield

Worcester

Providence

Plymouth

Pough-
keepsie

CONNECTICUT

Hartford

Chatham

New Haven

Nantucket

RHODE
ISLAND

New
York
City

Long
Island

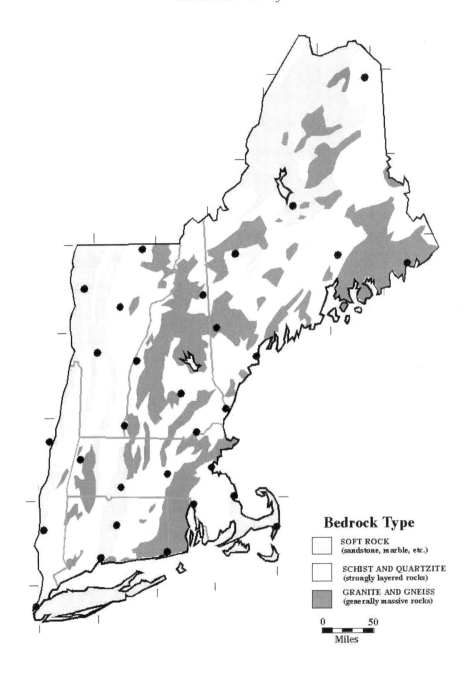

Bedrock Type

SOFT ROCK
(sandstone, marble, etc.)

SCHIST AND QUARTZITE
(strongly layered rocks)

GRANITE AND GNEISS
(generally massive rocks)

0   50
Miles

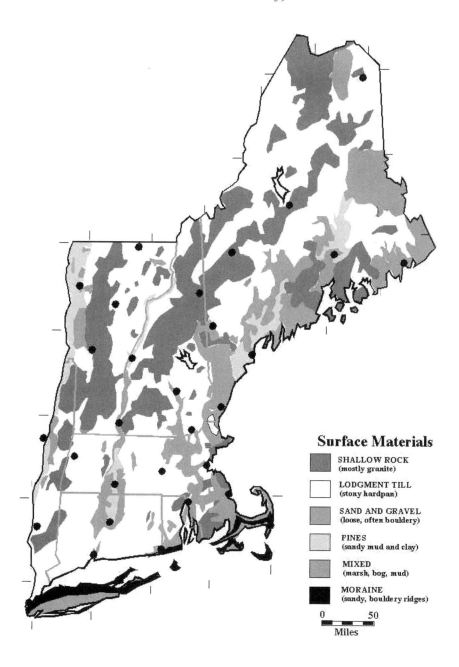

Surface Materials

SHALLOW ROCK
(mostly granite)

LODGMENT TILL
(stony hardpan)

SAND AND GRAVEL
(loose, often bouldery)

FINES
(sandy mud and clay)

MIXED
(marsh, bog, mud)

MORAINE
(sandy, bouldery ridges)

0   50
Miles

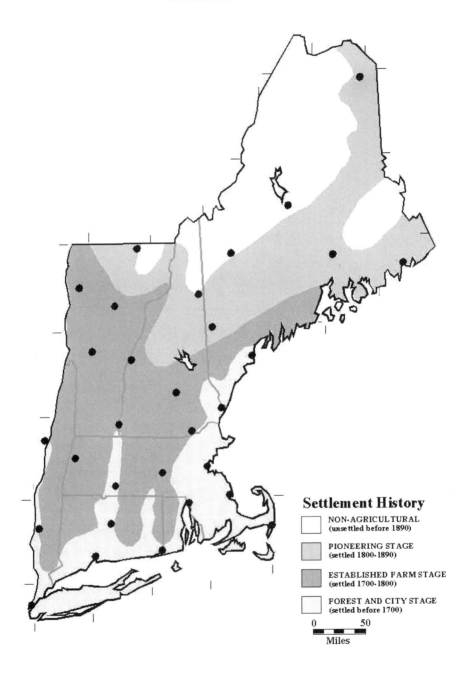

Settlement History

NON-AGRICULTURAL
(unsettled before 1890)

PIONEERING STAGE
(settled 1800-1890)

ESTABLISHED FARM STAGE
(settled 1700-1800)

FOREST AND CITY STAGE
(settled before 1700)

0   50
Miles

Additional Resources

BOOKS

NEW ENGLAND GUIDEBOOKS

Sections of this book—particularly those dealing with rocks and minerals, life on walls, topography, settlement history, and stone-wall tourism—can be enhanced by using other specialty travel and nature guides to the New England region, available from your favorite bookstore. For the best general guide to natural history, I recommend the National Audubon Society's *Field Guide to New England* (New York: Alfred A. Knopf, 1998), which provides an excellent introduction to the region's weather, stars, birds, mammals, flowers, trees, fish, and shoreline life. For more specific guides to local geology in Massachusetts, New Hampshire, and Vermont (and hopefully the other states in the near future), I recommend the *Roadside Geology Guides* (Missoula, Mt: Mountain Press, 1987–2002).

SCIENTIFIC REFERENCES

Jackson, Julia A. *Glossary of Geology.* 4th ed. Alexandria, Va.: American Geological Institute, 2002.
> *The definitive reference for geological terms in all subdisciplines.*

Marshak, Stephen. *Essentials of Geology.* New York: W. W. Norton, 2004.
> *Recommended text for basic geology. Separate chapters for all major subdisciplines.*

LANDSCAPES

Allport, Susan. *The Stone Walls of New England and New York.* Illustrated by David Howell. New York: W. W. Norton, 1990.
> *The first contemporary overview of stone walls, especially from the historical and literary perspective.*

Cronon, William. *Changes in the Land: Indians, Colonists and the Ecology of New England.* New York: Farrar, Straus and Giroux, 1983.
    Groundbreaking text on settlement and environmental change in New England, especially during the colonial epoch.

Foster, David R., and J. F. O'Keefe. *New England Forests through Time: Insights from the Harvard Forest Dioramas.* Cambridge, Mass.: Harvard University Press, 2000.
    Overview of vegetation change associated with land clearing, agriculture, forestry, and abandonment.

Gardner, Kevin. *The Granite Kiss: Traditions and Techniques of Building New England Stone Walls.* Woodstock, Vt.: Countryman Press, W. W. Norton, 2001.
    Construction techniques and commentary from the point of view of the stonemason.

Hayward, Gordon. *Stone in the Garden: Inspiring Designs and Practical Projects.* New York: W. W. Norton, 2001.
    A photo-illustrated guide for designing with stone.

Larkin, Jack. *The Reshaping of Everyday Life, 1790–1840.* New York: Harper and Row, 1988.
    A focused look at cultural attitudes at the farm/village scale during the time when most stone walls were being built.

Lenney, Christopher J. *Sightseeking: Clues to the Landscape History of New England.* Hanover, N.H.: University Press of New England, 2003.
    Survey of cultural processes that shaped the land, with an emphasis on rural architecture.

Russell, Howard. *A Long, Deep Furrow: Three Centuries of Farming in New England.* Hanover, N.H.: University Press of New England, 1976.
    A definitive review of the regional history of agriculture and its relationship to stone walls.

Thorson, Kristine, and Robert Thorson. *Stone Wall Secrets.* Gardiner, Me.: Tilbury-house Publishing, 1998.
    Illustrated story used to help children explore stone walls and appreciate their hidden values.

Thorson, Robert M. *Stone by Stone: The Magnificent History in New England's Stone Walls.* New York: Walker & Company, 2002.

A narrative history of stone walls written by a geologist from the archaeological perspective.

Wessels, Tom. *Reading the Forested Landscape: A Natural History of New England.* Woodstock, Vt.: Countryman Press, 1999.
Detective work on landscape reconstruction with an emphasis on forest history.

Whitney, Gordon G. *From Coastal Wilderness to Fruited Plain: A History of Environmental Change in Temperate North America from 1500 to the Present.* Cambridge, England: Cambridge University Press, 1994.
Scholarly overview of land settlement and ecologic impact, particularly after colonial times.

MAGAZINE

Saver, Peter. "Placemarks: Stone Walls," *Orion*, Vol. 11, No. 1, pp. 57–60. Winter 1992.

MAPS

Bennison, Allan P. *Geological Highway Map, Northeastern Region.* Tulsa, Oklahoma: American Association of Petroleum Geologists, 1995.
Overview of bedrock geology with special sections on geologic history, collecting localities, and battlefields. Available from AAPG, PO Box 979, Tulsa, OK 74101.

Soller, David R. *Map I-1970-A., scale 1:1,000,000.* (Map showing thickness and character of Quaternary sediments in the glaciated United States east of the Rocky Mountains.) Washington D.C.: U.S. Geological Survey Miscellaneous Investigations Series, 1993.
Overview of surface geology with an emphasis on glacial features such as drumlins, meltwater pathways, glacial lakes, and moraines.

Gerlach, Arch C., ed. *The National Atlas of the United States of America.* Washington, D.C.: U.S. Geological Survey, 1970.
A convenient, one-volume source for maps showing the soils, geology, climate, land use, and settlement history of New England and the rest of the United States.

INTERNET SITES

Association of American State Geologists, http://www.kgs.ukans.edu/AASG/
AASG.html

> *Each state has a geological survey, usually within its natural resources administration. These are the places to go for specific information about the geology and land use of areas at the scale of towns and individual properties. There is usually an information officer available to help you with questions and to sell maps and other materials.*

National Geophysical Data Center (NGDC), http://www.ngdc.noaa.gov/ngdcinfo/
onlineaccess.html

> *This federally maintained site is an archive of information about the topography, magnetism, gravity, relief, climate, and so on for all parts of New England, accessible by state. I particularly recommend the shaded relief topographic maps.*

Stone Wall Initiative (SWI), http://stonewall.uconn.edu

> *This is the home page for the Stone Wall Initiative, a clearinghouse and information center for New England's stone walls with an emphasis on their appreciation, investigation, education, and preservation. A good first contact for questions about exploring stone walls. Contains supplementary material for this book.*

United States Geological Survey (USGS), http://www.usgs.gov/

> *The USGS is part of the U.S. Department of the Interior; it does for the nation what state surveys do for individual states. It's the leading national agency for obtaining geological information, and a public information officer is available to answer questions.*

Tools and Equipment

Although no special equipment is needed to explore stone walls, several inexpensive items may be helpful.

Magnifying lens: Get a rugged one capable of magnifying at least 10 power. It will help you identify specific crystals within the stones, as well as tiny features on their surfaces, ranging from glacial chattermarks to the reproductive parts of lichens.

Binoculars: Oddly enough, a good pair of binoculars is useful because many walls may stand on private property, or lurk behind brambles you want to avoid. Binoculars will help you identify stone shapes and architectural details from a distance.

Measuring pole and probe: Any walking stick, cane, or pole can also serve as a measuring device for stone walls, and as a probe to poke around in the flanking apron. I recommend a shoulder-high pole of wood or plastic pipe. Mark it off at a height of 2 feet (the arbitrary minimum for an unstacked wall), then at closer intervals, down to 6 inches or even every inch in the lowermost foot. With such a device you can easily measure the width of walls and the dimensions of large stones. The base of the stick can also be used as a probe to locate fallen stones in the litter and brush, especially if it is narrow and if you have attached a metal tip to it.

Nature guide: There is plenty of life on and near walls that is part of their exploration. I recommend using the *National Audubon Society's Field Guide to New England* as a one-volume resource.

Geological map: This will help you identify which rock units are present in your area. To obtain one, simply contact the appropriate state geological survey listed by the American Association of State Geologists (see "Internet Sites," above).

Camera: Photographs, especially digital photographs, are the most convenient, accurate way to document and share images of stone walls. I recommend using a U.S. penny as a common scale in any close-ups.

Notebook: I recommend a hardcover surveyor's notebook, available in many office-supply stores and university bookstores. On the inside cover I recommend taping a copy of your stone-wall life list and any other charts and tables.

Classification Key

This section gives you a proper name for any stone wall (or related stone object), assuming you are familiar with the terminology. To work your way through the key, simply answer each question with a yes (**Y**) or no (**N**) answer; the answer no always directs you to another question. After each answer, move to the next level inside that section; for example, a question at level **N1** will send you either to answer **Y2** or to **N2**, and so forth. Repeat the process until you arrive at a name in capital letters. This takes a little practice. For convenience, the labels for all answers are in boldface; those at even-numbered levels are in italics.

There are two parts to the key. Part I gives you the class of stone object within the stone domain. Once you have the correct class, move to the following key for that particular class in Part II.

PART I
KEY TO STONE CLASSES

Feature consists of a single isolated stone distinct from its surroundings?
    Y1: Class NOTABLE STONE
    N1: Concentration of stones is four or more times longer than wide?
        Y2: Stones are continuous AND either stacked OR more than knee (2 ft) high?
            Y3 Class STONE WALL
            N3: Class STONE LINE
        N2: Class STONE CONCENTRATION

PART II
KEY TO CLASS STONE WALLS

Small (typically less than 40-foot) above-grade wall built as part of a confined space?

Y1: Family CONFINEMENT WALL

Small, unroofed, AND fencelike?

    Y2: Type STONE PEN (pound, corral, yard)

    N2: Roofed?

        Y3: Type STONE CHAMBER

        N3: Type RING WALLS (fire rings, stone circles)

N1: Stands above ground surface more or less evenly on both sides AND lacks a wedge of fill to one side?

    Y2: Family FREESTANDING WALL

Single row of large stones abutting each other?

        Y3: Type ABUTTING WALL (boulder, rock slab, stone pale)

        N3: Concentration of stones dumped, rather than stacked or laid?

            Y4: Type STONE BAND (wavy, beaded)

            N4: Stones stacked or laid in single line?

                Y5: Type SINGLE WALL (cordwood, lace, cannonball)

                N5: Stacked in two lines (slanting inward) AND no unnecessary width?

                    Y6: Type DOUBLE WALL (ornate, quarrystone-capped, quarrystone, copestone, turreted, guard)

                    N6: Type BROAD WALL (disposal, once-again, walking)

    N2: Stands above ground surface AND has a wedge of fill?

        Y3: Family IMPOUNDMENT WALL

Built across valley and stream (typically short and high)?

        Y4: Type MILL DAM

        N4: Built parallel to valley and stream?

            Y5: Type STONE DIKE (or levee)

            N5: Type POOLING Wall

        N3: Elevates land or soil on two or more sides?

        Y4: Family RAISING WALL

Walls built to span a stream?

        Y5: Type BRIDGING WALL (stone bridge, culvert)

N5: Built to raise working or transportation surface above low/ wet ground or shallow water?

    Y6: Type RAISED LAND WALL (causeway, groin, jetty, pier, edge-of-fill)

    N6: Type RAISED BED WALL (landscaping)

N4: Strong, level top built to support a building?

    Y5: Family FOUNDATION WALL (cellar, building, barn, house, outbuilding)

    N5: Family FLANKING WALL

    Designed principally to protect land from erosion?

    Y6: Type ARMORING WALL (riprap, facing, sea, stream-bank, chute)

    N6: Type RETAINING WALL (below-grade, above-grade, false retaining, well guards)

KEY TO CLASS STONE LINES

Stones abut each other?

    Y1: Family STONE LINE

    N1: Gaps are shorter than the stones?

    Y2: Family GAPPED STONE LINE

    N2: Family DOTTED STONE LINE (boulder dots, cobble dots, rock dots)

KEY TO CLASS STONE CONCENTRATIONS

One stone thick?

    Y1: Family STONE SURFACES

    Laid or occurring flat on the ground?

    Y2: Type PAVEMENT (tiled, cobblestone)

    N2: Type SLOPE VENEERS

    N1: Built (laid or stacked) above the ground?

    Y2: Family STONE UPRIGHTS

    Built to support weight from below?

    Y3: Type STONE PILLARS

N3: Built to vent smoke from a fire?

> **Y4:** Type CHIMNEY
>
> **N4:** Freestanding and supports a span?
>
> > **Y5:** Type STONE SPAN (lintels, arches)
> >
> > **N5:** Type STONE MONUMENT

N2: Family STONE PILE (not built; either dumped or tossed)

Isolated from any other stone feature?

> **Y3:** Type FREESTANDING PILE (simple, infill, burial mound, ring pile, stone rosette)
>
> **N3:** Type ATTACHED PILE (corner pile, flanking pile, topping pile, slab pile)

KEY TO CLASS NOTABLE STONES

Human movement or modification proven?

> **Y1:** Large, elongate stone with unstable center of gravity (not gravestone)?
>
> **Y2:** Family STANDING STONE
>
> Isolated and generally rough-shaped?
>
> > **Y3:** Type STONE OBELISKS
> >
> > **N3:** Type STONE POSTS (usually positioned and shaped)
>
> **N2:** Unornamented (not modified or manufactured in any way)?
>
> > **Y3:** Family PLACED STONE
> >
> > **N3:** Family MODIFIED STONE
> >
> > Old grinding stones?
> >
> > > **Y4:** Type GRINDING STONE (millstone, sharpening stone)
> > >
> > > **N4:** Type MONUMENT STONE (gravestone, carved stone)

N1: Family GLACIAL ERRATIC

Life List of Walls

Use this following list for all of your hikes, visits, and explorations.

Check off each type of stone wall as you encounter it.

Type/Subtype	Location	Date
FREESTANDING WALLS		
Stone bands		
❏ Standard	_____	_____
❏ Wavy stone band	_____	_____
❏ Beaded stone band	_____	_____
Single Walls		
❏ Standard	_____	_____
❏ Cordwood wall	_____	_____
❏ Lace wall	_____	_____
❏ Cannonball wall	_____	_____
Double Walls		
❏ Standard	_____	_____
❏ Ornate Double Walls	_____	_____
❏ Quarrystone-capped wall	_____	_____
❏ Quarrystone wall	_____	_____
❏ Copestone wall	_____	_____
❏ Turreted wall	_____	_____
❏ Guard wall	_____	_____
Broad Walls		
❏ Disposal wall	_____	_____
❏ Once-again wall	_____	_____
❏ Walking wall	_____	_____
	_____	_____

Abutting Walls
    ☐ Boulder wall
    ☐ Rock slab wall
    ☐ Stone pale wall

FLANKING WALLS
  Retaining Walls
    ☐ Below-grade retaining wall
    ☐ Above-grade retaining wall
    ☐ False retaining wall
    ☐ Well guard
  Armoring Walls
    ☐ Riprap wall
    ☐ Facing wall

RAISING WALLS
    ☐ Raised bed
    ☐ Raised land
      • Edge of fill
      • Causeway
      • Stone groin
      • Stone jetty
      • Stone pier
    ☐ Bridging wall
      • Culvert wall
      • Stone bridge wall

IMPOUNDMENT WALLS
    ☐ Stone dike
    ☐ Mill dam
    ☐ Pooling wall

FOUNDATION WALLS
    ☐ Cellar hole
    ☐ Barn foundation
    ☐ House foundation
    ☐ Outbuilding foundation

Confinement Walls

Stone Pens

❑ Town pound _____ _____

❑ Stone corral _____ _____

Ring Walls

❑ Fire ring _____ _____

❑ Stone circle _____ _____

Stone chamber _____ _____

INDEX

Page numbers in italics refer to illustrations.